I started to read *Unpacking for the Journey* the day Hurricane Katrina so violently began to unpack New Orleans, Biloxi and many other coastal towns. As pictures of people being stripped of family members, friends and of all their worldly possessions filled my eyes, these homilies became my touchstone, and my way of attempting to make some meaning of the losses.

For me, a recovering "pack rat," the primary message in this book is that we depend far too heavily on physical, mental and even spiritual things to protect us. We hoard that which can disappear in the flash of a flood, the heat of fire, the fickleness of the world market, the results of a lab test. Instead of relying on what we have accumulated to make ourselves feel safe Father Eifler counsels that "we must begin to unpack all the stuff we desperately rely on," whether they be attitudes, biases, world views, or even more mundane things like ever-larger houses, cars and retirement funds.

In each homily Fr. Eifler draws on his depth of experience and the life stories of those he knows and loves, to explain and to remind us of the best news – that we are the children of a passionately loving God who calls us to loving relationship with one another, who knows our needs and would shower us with even more gifts if we didn't already have our fists so full of stuff we don't need!

> — *Jane M. Thibault, Ph.D.*
> *Associate Clinical Professor*
> *School of Medicine University of Louisville*
> *Author:* 10 Gospel Promises for Later Life

Father Jerry Eifler's latest collection of homilies reveals much about the author—well-read, widely-traveled, artistic—but it reveals even more about the human condition.

Using as his backdrop his many encounters with people—friends and acquaintances as well as total strangers—Father Jerry confronts the profound life-themes of love, peace, justice and forgiveness, using examples from the lives of ordinary people doing ordinary things.

He faces his readers head on with the hard choices they must make on their journey to a rewarding, satisfying and spiritually healthy life; give up the anger, the grudge, the pretense—in other words, give up the "baggage." This is easier said than done, but it is the roadmap for the readers' successful journey through life.

> — *Honorable Romano L. Mazzoli*
> *Member, U.S. Congress, 1971-1995*

UNPACKING
for the JOURNEY

JERRY EIFLER

BUTLER BOOKS

*I dedicate this book to the faith community
of St. Frances of Rome, Louisville, Kentucky, as well as those
who have walked beside me and shared their journey.*

ISBN 1-884532-70-5

Printed in Canada through Four Colour Imports
Louisville, KY

For information contact Butler Books
P.O.Box 7311, Louisville, KY 40207
502-897-9393
billbutler@insightbb.com
www.butlerbooks.com

With deep appreciation for their support, I thank
Jo Anne Hohman for her honesty and editing skills;
Martha Martin, Alice Baldwin, Pat Hohman and
Carolyn Breen for recommending and selecting the
content; Paul Weber, Rev. Al Shands, Congressman
Ron Mazzoli, Jane Thibault, G. Wade Rowatt, and
Peggy Donnelly for their friendship and insights;
and a special thanks to Margaret Williams whose
dedication and perseverance made this book possible.

Preface

I would never have agreed to write a preface to a book of homilies if I had not read Father Jerry Eifler's first book, *Linger and Be Available*. It was a delightfully insightful trek through Sacred Scripture and one pastor's experience of life. So of course I jumped at the opportunity to write the preface for *Unpacking for the Journey*. The title itself provides a clue to Father Jerry's subtle sense of humor. For members of St. Frances of Rome Catholic Church, however, there's another bit of amusement. For years Father Jerry has led tour groups all over Europe and the Holy Land. He likes to travel and is definitely an expert packer.

But this book is not about European travels; it is a series of reflections on religion, scripture and this journey called life. It is about letting go, not of material things as such, but of psychological and spiritual baggage—fears, resentments, false dogmas, judging others, control. When you stop to think about it, we all carry a lot of excess baggage that hinders God from entering and fulfilling our lives.

Each of the thirty-eight homilies is about four pages in length, and ties together scriptural readings with universal human experiences, often illustrated with stories from the lives of people Father Jerry has met along his way. I found the entries a perfect length for beginning meditation. They are also about the right length for reading out loud to someone else. Even the titles give us pause. Two of my favorites are "Where have We Laid Jesus?" and "The Porcupine Homily."

If I had to crystallize a theme for the volume, it would be: "God's great love for us, despite our human weaknesses." In fact, these homilies bring to mind a book that had a profound impact on me when I was much younger. It was by a French Jesuit, Henri de Lubac, entitled, *The Splendor of the Church*. One quotation I copied and saved is this:

"The Church is no exclusive Club for spiritual geniuses

or supermen; No academy for the clever. In fact, she is the very opposite. The warped, the sham, and the wretched of every kind, crowd together into her, together with the whole host of the Mediocre, who feel especially at home in her and everywhere set the tone of things…

But there is no private Christianity, and if we are to accept the Church we must take her as she is, in her human day-to-day reality just as much as in her divine and eternal ideality; for separation of the two is impossible. We have to push to its conclusion the logic of the Incarnation by which the Divine adapts to human weakness."

Unpacking for the Journey expands on that insight in sometimes surprising, but always interesting, ways. I hope you enjoy reading these as much as I have.

— *Paul J. Weber, Ph.D.*
Distinguished Teaching Professor of Political Science
University of Louisville

Author's Note: Since writing this Preface, Paul Weber completed his final journey into eternal life on October 9, 2005.

Introduction

The gift of life from birth to death is seen as a journey. God made us a promise that he will take care of us, protect us, and bring us home to be with him forever at the end of our journey. But how do we get there? We begin by learning what to take on our journey and what to leave behind.

Viewing life as a journey—with a lot of stops and obstacles along the way—we begin to realize that we collect a lot of "stuff." It is a natural tendency to become a pack rat, either spiritually, physically or mentally. This prevents us from truly seeing others and our purpose in life.

As life goes on, this stuff we carry within us can get pretty heavy and weigh us down. So we attempt to lighten our baggage. We try to put aside our hasty judgments, our need to always be right, and our preconceptions about "those other people." We also try to put aside our guilt for the times we fail. The emphasis is on trying; because change doesn't come easily to any of us.

There are some who say that our task as human beings is not learning to be spiritual as much as learning to be human. I think God is going to hold us accountable, not so much for our spiritual attempts, but for our human attempts in living life.

So we must begin to unpack all the stuff we desperately rely on. As Jesus suggested to his disciples: *Do not carry a walking staff, or a traveling bag; wear no sandals...* or anything else that may be a distraction from our ultimate goal of being embraced by a loving, prodigal, extravagant God.

In reading this book, I hope you will find encouragement and points for meditation that will help you unpack for your journey.

Note: It should be understood that these Sunday homilies were originally heard in story-telling form, and then transcribed into the written word. Any quotes from theologians, authors or others are paraphrased and not verbatim.

Table of Contents

A Trek Out of Darkness

Hosea 6:3-6
Matthew 9:9-13

The last words of the Gospel this morning set the theme for the homily. These words were taken by Jesus from Hosea the Prophet. He said, "I desire mercy, not sacrifice. I desire the knowledge of God, not holocaust." These words describe the whole mission of Jesus.

In the Gospel today, we have the story of a beginning relationship between Jesus and a man named Matthew. I have a hunch that all of Jesus' disciples and apostles were chosen, not for their self-righteousness, but for their humanness and their sinfulness. What Jesus brings to us (to them) is not self-righteousness, but love and the knowledge of God.

One of the most dramatic paintings that I have ever seen in my life, and one that I seek out whenever I am in Rome, is a painting that is entitled *The Call of Matthew* by Caravaggio. It was painted around 1600. It is in the Church of San Luigi dei Francesi (St. Louis of France.)

It was rejected initially by the Church because Caravaggio painted Matthew with dirty bare feet and dirty hands, sitting at a table with other tax collectors and merchants. On the right hand of the painting, out of the darkness, comes the finger of Jesus pointing to Matthew. Matthew sort of sheepishly looks up and is somewhat embarrassed.

This man, Matthew, was a tax collector. He was Jewish. The Jewish people despised him because he would base his salary on the amount of tax that the merchants brought into and out of the gate in Jerusalem. It was up to Matthew to charge whatever he wanted to charge. On the other hand, Matthew worked for the Romans. The Romans had complete control of the land and they didn't respect this Jew for being a tax collector either.

Nobody trusted Matthew. He simply went to his post day after day and levied taxes. He wasn't accepted by the Jews or the Romans. He just existed. The more we know about Matthew, the more we find that he had no dignity whatsoever. He didn't feel good about himself. He was caught in a bind and he couldn't get out of it. I think that Jesus and Matthew saw each other periodically. A glance here or there, but never a conversation. Matthew would be embarrassed by any conversation because what would a teacher like Jesus be doing talking to a tax collector?

But Jesus knew him. And on this particular day, as recorded in the scriptures, Jesus went to Matthew and perhaps for the first time, their eyes really met. They gazed upon each other: Matthew, embarrassed and somewhat frightened, and Jesus, with love. Jesus said, "Matthew, come follow me."

Scripture says that on this night, Jesus had dinner in Matthew's house. It really upset everyone. The Pharisees, the Scribes, the tax collectors and other people said, "What's going on here? Why is Matthew, the one we despise, involved with Jesus?"

But when Jesus extended the invitation to him, Matthew replied, "I am Matthew, a sinner. Come to my house." Those words were the first words that Matthew spoke on his spiritual journey that eventually took him out of this experience of self-doubt, of pain, of indignity. It was only because of the invitation to dinner that Matthew had the opportunity to begin his trek out of darkness.

We can take great journeys to find what we could really find at home within ourselves—deep, honest spirituality. It is only when we can afford to be honest with ourselves that we begin this journey out of darkness. Many of us carry a lot of things that we need to get rid of. More and more, society is offering us illusive enticements that we so readily buy into. It could be the need to just amass stuff to surround ourselves with, often to camouflage pain. It could be alcohol, drugs, sex, pornography.

In 1935, there was a doctor from Akron, Ohio and a

stockbroker in New York who had a common problem. Their problem was that of addiction. Their families had lectured them. Their friends had talked sense to them. They had gone off to be cured, but nothing really happened. Nothing happened until they began to set aside everything that they had learned, and, like Matthew, started to become teachable.

As many of you may know, these two men were instrumental in beginning the AA Program for people with addictions to alcohol. From the AA Program, many similar programs have evolved, including a program for children, parents, spouses or friends of alcoholics, and for people with addictions to gambling or food. Just in this city of Louisville alone, there are over 300 meetings a week for AA, to say nothing of the many meetings for all the other programs.

What the addicted founders of AA first discovered was that in the human experience, only when they found themselves down and out, and "sick and tired of being sick and tired," and only then, were they most apt to really respond to the invitation to come to the table of the Lord. Because, up to that point, they had enough tricks in their kitbag to keep themselves afloat.

When we find ourselves bottoming out, then we can find ourselves ripe for the *presence* of God. We are able to turn our lives over to God, just as Matthew did. Matthew left his post as the tax collector and he became a follower of Jesus. He bathed, he found friends, he was accepted, and ultimately Matthew became one of the greatest apostles of Christ. All because he accepted the invitation, "Come follow me." Implied in that invitation is, "I will give you help, I will free you. I will take away your doubt and your pain."

My friends, you and I are the ones who have to take the step. The invitation is always extended. But we have to take that step to let God be in our lives. In doing so, then we understand what sacrifice is, but we also understand what love is. We are able to share love with each other. We understand what the knowledge of God is. Not God as a tyrant, but God as an extravagant lover who picks us up out of our own humanness and gives us the opportunity for dignity.

Every time I go to Rome, I spend time just looking at that painting because I think it is so real. It is real in my life and it is real in the lives of many other people. We gather around the table with our friends and our cohorts, we stay there with dirty feet and hands and we talk about the stuff that occupies our existence. Over on the side, there is this figure in the dark with a shining hand coming out and he is pointing to one of us. In my case, he is pointing to me. He is saying, "Come follow me." And that's when life begins. We all have an invitation to the table of the Lord today. We come to the table, free of burden, free of fear, free of accusation. We come with a sense of well-being and serenity, knowing that we are loved by God, and that he calls each one of us, not out of righteousness, but out of the pain of sin, and gives us dignity. Listen well for that invitation, because we all need it. And I might add, don't be late for dinner.

From the Dogma to the Dance

Proverbs 8: 22-31
Romans 5: 1-5
John 16: 12-15

In a letter to a friend, American author Flannery O'Connor suggested, "Dogma is only the gateway to contemplation and is an instrument of freedom and not of restriction. It preserves mystery for the human mind." This month we introduce two feasts of dogmas: the Feast of the Holy Trinity, celebrated today, and Corpus Christi, or the Feast of the Eucharist, which we celebrate next Sunday. But, what is dogma and what does it have to do with the ever-changing seasons of our world and our lives?

As defined by the church, dogma is a doctrine promulgated with the highest authority and solemnity. Today, we are invited to embrace the mystery freely and fully, not only with our minds, but even more so, with our hearts and souls.

Throughout the centuries, many have attempted to explain the dogma and enunciate the mystery of the Trinity in a variety of ways. There have been many right-brain illustrations and symbols of Trinity. One that is most familiar is the story of St. Patrick and the three-leaf clover. But there are also the equilateral triangle, three intertwined circles and three fish in a circle.

On the other hand, there are people who have well-developed left sides of the brain, and they delve into the mystery. We have a tremendous list of significant theologians and scholars all the way up to the present day, who have delved into understanding the mystery. Perhaps the one that we accept and are more familiar with than any of the others is Thomas Aquinas. He talks about the tremendous love of God, the Creator/God, the Mother/Father God, and their projected love, which created the Son. The Son, in loving the Father, created the Holy Spirit.

For you and for me, we know the Trinity to be God the Creator, Jesus the Redeemer, and the Holy Spirit, the Sanctifier. That is our tradition. That is what we know about the Trinity. But neither the symbols of the right side of the brain, nor the theology and the writings of the left side of the brain take us any place. All the knowledge in the world isn't going to affect anything. It is only when you and I, as Flannery O'Conner said, step through the gateway into the concept of contemplation, that we find understanding.

Now, you don't have to be a monk to be a contemplative. Quite the contrary. Once you become aware of it, then contemplation is yours. It is prayer. It is our ability to enter into a concept that we really don't understand, but that faith dictates that we believe, and that we want to believe. All through scripture, in the Old and New Testaments, we have these little vignettes, these little insights, these little seeds, that can activate our minds and hearts to be able to enter into contemplation.

One that is very strong for me on this Feast of the Trinity is the end of our reading from Proverbs. The writer of Proverbs talks about the creation of the world. Proverbs says that when God created the clouds, and the water, and the mountains and all that we know as nature, "I was there." Then God danced on his creation, and he looked upon this human race and he "was very pleased." What a beautiful statement.

A dancing God! Has that ever been part of your prayer life? That is what Flannery O'Connor means. Take a morsel like that and go through the gateway of dogma into contemplation. Think about God dancing on his world, in creation and in the mountains and in the valleys and in the sunrise and in the sunset. Then he looks on his prized creation and he sees you and me, human beings, with our freedom, with the gifts and abilities that have been given to us. "And God was very pleased." To me, that is a strong motive for prayer. To find a quiet place and enter into the mystery of what we are talking about today, the Trinity.

This is what we are to do with our theology and our dogma and the tenets of our faith. Many times we intellectualize them. We just go through Church history books and theology books and try to memorize every line and every fact in the book. But that is not prayer. That is not contemplation. Prayer is recognizing a mystery and making it part of our spiritual journey. When we do, then it really doesn't matter if we understand it or not. The mystery of the dogma is necessary for our faith. We recognize that there is something we don't understand and that we just have to take on faith, and we believe it to be part of the unknown of God.

What does God look like? We think about the symbols on the right side of the brain. We consider the Trinity and we think of God the Father as the old man with the white beard. We think about Jesus Christ as the one who walked around with long hair. And how we ever came up with the idea of a dove for the Holy Spirit, I will never know. But it not important that we have a fixed concept of what the Father, Son and Holy Spirit look like. What is important is that we recognize the love that God has for us, and the invitation that is extended to us to come and play in his creation. Our faith gives us that opportunity to have God look at you and me, as we are, with the stuff we brought with us this morning - our fears, our joys, our sadness or whatever it might be - and know that he is pleased. Now, that is real prayer.

On your spiritual journey don't be afraid to enter into contemplation. Find something that speaks to you in the Word and take it with you into the mystery. In that place, we have to become dependent upon God. Just sit there with it and let God speak to you. Therein you and I are enriched. And then we come back out of that place to the gateway that O'Connor refers to, and we are better off. We are stronger. We are able to say that the Church will be better tomorrow than it is today. You and I will be blessed more tomorrow than we are today. There will be a continual unfolding of God's healing love and power for eternity.

So we look forward to celebrating this mystery of the Trinity when we see it as the gateway to a gift that is given to us by God. So if you hear the invitation to go play in God's world, do it! I'm planning to be there myself.

Don't Miss the Parade

John 10:11-18

Today is the Feast of the Good Shepherd. You need to put this idea into context, which I will briefly do. In the old days, before the time of Christ, the shepherd was considered an important leader of the community. He was a man of dignity. He was able to provide food, clothing and guidance for the people of his tribe. If you look back in our history you will find that Abraham, Isaac and Ezekiel were shepherds. Most of the people at that time were migrants. They were always on the road.

By the time they settled in Jerusalem after the second destruction of the city, their claim to wealth and power changed. The role of the shepherd was minimal now. He was lord of the lowly. He was surpassed in the line of dignity only by the tax collector—Matthew, for example, who worked for the Roman government.

When John wrote this particular gospel that speaks of the Good Shepherd, it was about 70 years after the time of Christ. By that time, the whole concept of the theology of the time was different. So what he was presenting to the people was the person who was considered the least among many, and comparing the shepherd's role to that of Christ, who brought light, life and salvation to the people.

We are aware of the "classifications" that we find in our society. They have been around forever. Many times we just accept that and go on about our business, not particularly recognizing the uniqueness of individuals. That is to our detriment, not to our credit. We must remember that, as stated in the reading this morning, we are all loved uniquely as individuals; in the eyes of God, one is not better than the other.

But now on to what I really want to share with you today - an experience I had during the Derby festivities. I had a couple of house guests from Florida, so I took them down to the parade on Thursday night, rain and all. We had great seats, right at Fourth and Broadway. So we settled in to watch the parade and take in all the sights. Right in front of us were four young girls and a young boy. They were quite excited and the girls were really getting into the music of the bands and were swinging and dancing with great hoopla. Boy, could they dance!

Then, there was the little boy. This little boy looked like he was bored to death. He was looking around and he was picking on things and going back and forth, crawling over my legs and that kind of thing. I looked at him and I said, "Do you dance?" And he said, "Nope." Then I said, "Are these girls your sisters?" "Yep" he answered. I said, "They surely know how to dance, don't they?" "Yep" he replied.

That was about the gist of the conversation. After we had broken the ice and some time had passed, the boy looked at me and said, "Is there a lot more to this parade?" I looked up the street to see and answered, "Yes, there is a lot more."

"Is there a lot, lot more to this parade?"

"Yes, there is a lot, lot more!"

"Is there a lot, lot, lot more?"

This time I answered, "I'm afraid so." He then turned to his sisters and said, "There is a lot, lot, lot more to this parade!" They couldn't have cared less. They were out there doing the boogie, doing their thing.

I've thought about this little boy often during this past week. I've thought about the fact that he didn't dance, and he didn't really look at what was passing by in front of him. He was so preoccupied about what was going to happen next and so caught up in waiting for it to be over that he missed the parade. He didn't see a thing that was going on. He didn't allow himself to get into the moment. What was he doing? He was killing time. When I told him that there was a lot, lot, lot more of the parade, you could see the expression on his face change. He wasn't a happy camper.

The thought has occurred to me that so many times, as you and I live out our lives, we are either preoccupied with what has happened in the past or we are wondering about what is going to happen in the future. Sometimes we are so involved in this that we too miss the parade. We talk about the "good old times." You and I know, in reality, that there is no such thing as the good old times. When people ask us if we want to take part in the activities of the good old days, whether it be hygiene, or food, or travel, or recreation, we usually say we don't want to do it. I must say that I get a big kick out of people who have never seen a Latin mass, but who tell me how much they miss a Latin mass! I often ask them why they like it so much and they will tell me that it "has such passion, such rhythm."

All this is often part of the figment of our imagination. You and I can do a number on ourselves about how good things *were*. When in reality, they weren't any better than they are now. And then, we look to the future. People get involved in the future and they are going to plan for this thing, that thing and the other thing. Many times, they miss the moment of being able to be with each other, to bond with each other, the moment for parents to listen to their children and for the children to listen to their parents. We miss so much when we become so preoccupied about what is going to happen next.

Not too long ago I was talking with an individual and I said, "Well, what are you going to do ten years from now, when you are thirty." And he said, "I would like to be a surgeon." So I said, "What are you doing now to make sure that you become a surgeon?" And he said, "Well, I go to school." I replied, "But you have been a lawn keeper for the last two years. How does that fit into your goal of being a surgeon?"

The point is that the future is contingent on what you and I do here and now. The only time that you and I have any responsibility before God is *now*. The ancient writers during the first fourteen hundred years of Christianity always spoke of the eternal *nunc*. The *hic et nunc*—the here and now. They always counseled their people to be in the present moment, to let the past go, and not to make it a burden as we sometimes do because we carry blame and shame with it. We have to let all of that go.

The unconditional love that God has for us is now. And the future is contingent upon what we do now. So, if we are going to be able to get into the parade, so to speak, to appreciate the *now*, then we have to be conscious of it now. And we have to leave the rest of it up to God. The future will take care of itself. We will be fine. Because faith tells us that we will be fine.

And there's another thing that we have to do. We can't be idle spectators during the parade. We have to be like those little girls. We have to be willing to dance. We have to be willing to take part in it. We have to be willing to be absorbed in what we do now.

Many times we spend a lot of money traveling all over the place only to come back and look at the videos and the pictures of the place we visited and say, "Where was that? I think I took that picture but I don't remember where it was!" That's life. That's life for a lot of us because we don't give ourselves the gift of being present now.

We need to get into the dance. We need to step forward. We need to recognize the rhythm. We need to enjoy the sun that is coming in this door. We need to feel the breeze and smell the air after a rain. We need to be perceptive to life.

My friends, you and I can't afford to miss the parade. It has cost us too much to get there. We have to be willing to get into the dance, and when we do, we know where we are, we know what is happening all about us. Most of all, we discover that we are in an intimate relationship with our God and this is the only time we can enter into such a relationship. We can't enter into a relationship with God in the past, as we stand here now, nor in the future. It is only *hic et nunc*, here and now. And my friends, the *now* is truly eternal.

So don't miss the parade. It is unbelievable!

The Ultimate Gift

Exodus 20:1-17
1 Corinthians 1:22-25
John 2:13-15

The generosity of God is far greater than any tragedy or painful human experience that you and I might have to face. Perhaps you remember the story of the Green family from California, who in 1994 decided to go on a trip to Italy. They rented a car and planned to go through the hill towns as well as to the usual tourist spots. They initially had some great experiences until they were traveling in some rather desolate countryside, when they were ambushed by thieves. These thieves riddled the car with bullets.

The seven-year-old son was seriously injured. He was taken to a hospital where he died. The Greens decided that it would be appropriate to donate their son's vital organs for other patients who needed them. As a result of their gift, eight Italians were given new life through his eyes, heart, kidneys, liver, skin and lungs. This was unusual because it is not the custom in that part of the world.

As a result of this, the family found a great sense of satisfaction, because they knew that in a way, their son was living on in these eight people who received the organs. Later on, in 1999, Reg Green wrote a book as a result of the change of attitude the people showed. He found that many people were offering life-giving support to others in this fashion. The name of the book is *The Nicholas Effect*. It is sub-titled *A Boy's Gift to the World*. I have read a synopsis of the book and found it absolutely fascinating. Fascinating from the standpoint that the family was able to see the value in looking through the pain of the tragedy to be aware of the needs of others. Another aspect that I found interesting was the fact that other people then caught on to the value of doing this.

I also thought about the readings for this week. The first reading is the story of Abraham. When we read this story about God asking Abraham to sacrifice his son Isaac, we remember that Abraham was asked to give up the most precious entity that he had. Yet, Abraham trusted God. This passage has always been considered a foreshadowing of God's love for us in giving his Son to die on the cross on our behalf.

In reality, when you and I are faced with the death of a loved one and all that this brings about—the sense of loss, the sense of mourning, the sense of anger—it's incumbent upon us to hold on to this faith that Abraham demonstrated. The same faith that the Greens demonstrated in Italy.

This past week I was asked to go to the hospital to visit some friends of mine. I knew a young couple 40 years ago who were members of my teenage club. As things go, this attractive couple got engaged and they asked me to witness their wedding. Then, as the children came along, they asked me to baptize the children. When one of their daughters was planning to marry, they asked me to witness her wedding. Their other daughter plans to get married in April this year and I will be there. But the other day, the husband called and said, "It is time for you to come now." His wife has been battling cancer for eight years. So when I went over to the hospital, I had mixed emotions. These people are part of my life. I am part of their lives. All their events of living have been shared with me. I gave the mother the Anointing of the Sick. All the family was there. We prayed, and asked God's blessing. In a way, we reached back to Abraham, and sought what he found. A sense of security that only God can give.

Later, I took the husband aside and I said, "I have to ask you if you have given her permission to die." He said, "Yes. I did it last night." I have found that one of the greatest gifts a loved one can give another individual is permission to leave. Over a period of a long extended illness there is that need to stay alive. There is that energy, that expectation the patient many times has, to perform and to get well. It is impossible for them to do all this! So when my friend told his wife that he had always loved her, that their love was profound, that it would continue on, that she would always be with him, there was a sense of acceptance. Acceptance on her part and certainly an acceptance on his part.

I share this story with you this morning because I think it has to do with what Peter, James and John found on the mountaintop. I think that they found the reality of God there, never to be outdone in his gift. There was a sense of change, a sense of resignation, a sense of reality, and above all, there was a sense of gratitude. Gratitude to God for having had the opportunity to be part of the life of this particular individual.

When you and I express gratitude we also need to express joy. Joy and gratitude go hand in hand. You really can't say "I'm very grateful" with a sad face. I've often thought about Abraham, who, when God said, "Don't touch that boy" knew of the profound relationship he had with God. Paul is trying to tell his people that in the second reading, when he said, "God will never be outdone in generosity."

You and I have had to face the reality of death in our lives. We can either face it with anger or we can face it with grace and blessing. When we do, then there is a transformation that takes place, not only within ourselves, but also when we express our love to the person who is passing.

This morning, as we ponder these readings and events of life that we always face in death, may our prayer be one of gratitude and joy, because as Peter said, "It is good for us to be here."

Throw Away the Boxes

Ezekiel 2:2-5
2 Corinthians 12:7-10
Mark 6:1-6

In the readings that we have today, there are three examples of the prophet. The prophet was used by God to bring the message to his people, both in the Old and New Testaments and in our own time and space. We know from history that no one likes to be a prophet. It is a lousy job. The benefits of being a prophet are not that great!

That's what we find when we study Ezekiel, our prophet this morning. He didn't want the job. He tried to get out of it. But God said, "No, you will do this. You will speak to the Israelites." And so he did, at a great cost. It was humiliating for him. They ridiculed him. They took advantage of him. They didn't pay attention to him. It was a very difficult task indeed.

Then we look at the prophet Paul. Mostly we call Paul the Apostle of the Gentiles. But truly he was a prophet. He brought messages from God to the people. In this particular reading, Paul speaks out of his own personal problem. It is a problem that Paul has carried for many years. It is one that he has asked God to remove from him. Yet, God comes back and tells Paul, "My grace is sufficient for you. You must continue on. You'll be all right. Have faith in me."

Through the years, scripture scholars and theologians have speculated about what Paul's problem might have been. Some say he stuttered. Others say that he had epilepsy. Others say that it was some type of a sexual situation. Some say it was because he was short and bald. No one really knows what Paul's problem was. But we do know that Paul gives us a tremendous example of how to deal with life on life's terms.

Paul says, "When I am weak, I am strong." I think what he really means by that is that when you and I can embrace our own imperfections and weaknesses, then we make them our own and we no longer need to carry around the burden that we perceive this imperfection to be. There is a saying in the Twelve Step program that says "You are only as sick as your secrets." I think there is a lot of truth in that statement. When we have something that we perceive to be unacceptable in any form, then we guard that secret. You can only imagine how much emotional and spiritual energy we use to maintain that secret.

But when we are finally able to take it out into the bright day and we can admit the secret, it is no longer a secret. Most of the time when we admit to this fact, the response of the people is something like, "Well, why were you worrying about that? It is really not an issue." But for us, it is an issue. For Paul, it was an issue. Yet, when he learned to embrace his imperfections he found strength.

That made Paul a strong, aggressive individual. He went forth before the entire Gentile nation, and he preached the Word.

Next, we have Jesus as a prophet. Jesus came with a mission. The mission was from his father who asked him to preach the message of love. Yet, within his own hometown, within his own family and his extended family, he wasn't accepted. More than once Jesus went back to Nazareth and preached from the synagogue or read the scriptures, and he was ridiculed. One place in scripture it says, "He proved himself too much for them." In turn, they wanted to stone him. And scripture says, "Jesus walked right through their midst, never to return."

Clearly, Paul also changed residences. He moved to Capernaum. That is where he lived out his life. That was also the home of Peter, and the home of other colleagues in his ministry. Within our own relationships or in our own small world, we have the tendency to put each other in boxes, with preconceived notions about what the person ought to be, or the way they have always been or the way we used to know them back in high school. When an individual elects to change or to grow or to do something different, it's a threat. It is a threat to many people.

There is an interesting book that I often recommend. It is called *Conjoint Family Therapy*, by Helen Satir. It talks about the roles that people play in a family. When you look at it, everyone in the family has a role to play. There is a peacemaker. There is the identified patient. There is the one who has to be the entertainer. There is the one who just simply goes off and is quiet. All these roles are played, but when one person changes, it is a threat to everyone. I often think about people who decide to deal with addictions, like an addiction to alcohol. Let's say this individual has been addicted for many years. But he finds reason to change and he goes into a program and comes out sober. He is sober for a number of months perhaps.

If you watch the ebb and flow of the relationships you will find that there is something that begins to happen. What begins to happen is what we call sabotage. Others would come and say, "You know, so and so is doing so well on the program. It's been six months and she hasn't been drinking. But it is her birthday. It wouldn't hurt to serve her a drink today." But the individual knows so well that it would hurt her. There is that quiet effort to put the individual back into the box - the box of addiction.

What's that got to do with us? I think that we all do it. I think we all have these little boxes that we put everybody in and by golly, they better not get out of that little box! Because if they do, we will not feel comfortable.

A couple of examples: A couple of years ago I went to a St. X class reunion. We had our yearbooks out to see who was there, and we were trying to match the pictures with the 60+ year-old men. We were doing a pretty good job until one man came in and no one recognized him. And he had on his arm this absolutely, uh, I think the phrase is, *drop-dead-gorgeous woman*. We looked through the yearbook and we couldn't find him. We finally discovered that the individual was a person who did nothing in high school. Not one word was under his picture in the year book. And if you had to take a vote at that time of graduation, he would probably be the one least likely to succeed. That was our interpretation of this person. That's the box we had him in!

But many years passed. The individual changed and grew like most of the rest of us. When he came to our reunion, he came in his own Lear jet. The woman on his arm was indeed his wife. He was a successful shipping magnate up on the east coast. None of us could believe that this was the same individual we knew in high school.

At the book-signing event last month, one of my classmates from seminary days came to the celebration. He was absolutely blown away that I had written a book! I said, "What do you want me to put in the book?" Just write "Surprise!" He has called me four times since then to talk about the book. He said to his wife, "I can't believe Jerry wrote that book." She said, "Well, maybe he is a slow bloomer."

My point is, that when we deal with each other, we have to be willing to listen and to realize that the prophets are among us. Prophets from the standpoint of Ezekiel, or prophets from the standpoint of Paul, or prophets from the standpoint of Jesus. We all have something to say to each other. And we need to listen to each other. We simply can't categorize and set on the shelf individuals who are close to us. We have to be open. When we are open, we have the opportunity to learn, to reassess our own position, to be able to discover a new way of dealing with each other. It's simply not just neat little concepts and clear-cut ideas that we would like to have in the boxes.

In conclusion, I suppose that the sitcom most of us are familiar with, *All in the Family,* sort of sums it all up. When Archie Bunker was first on television, the entire American nation was glued to the TV. I've thought about that a lot and I've wondered if the reason why we liked Archie Bunker was because he could say what we have sometimes thought. He could murmur prejudices that we only think about. And we would laugh at him.

I can remember only one show that Archie starred in where he wasn't sarcastic about people all around the world. It was when Meathead and his wife had a little baby. There was a big argument in the show about getting the baby baptized. Meathead said, "Absolutely not. That baby is not going to be baptized." And Archie said, "That baby has got to be baptized!" So, one afternoon, Archie took the baby and went to the church. He pushed back the cover over the baptismal font and he took the baby and held it over the basin. He took the water and held it over the baby and looked up to heaven and said, "Now understand, God, this is just between you and me." And then he baptized the baby.

It is incumbent upon us to open our minds and our hearts to each other. To assume the roles that have been given to us. To free ourselves of the burdens that we feel are so unacceptable to other people. And to enjoy each other along the journey that has been given to us. I think that is the message of our readings today. One that causes us to pause and ponder about just where we are on this journey of life.

Eucharist: Repackaging Our Gifts

1 Corinthians 11:23-26

I feel like introducing myself to you this morning as Jerry Eifler, a priest in recovery from skepticism and anger. The reason I say this is because I told you last week that I was going to go to the Annual Presbyteral Assembly, which is a meeting of all the priests in the diocese, over at St. Meinrad. I wasn't necessarily looking forward to going to this four-day assembly because I have been there many times before. I decided three years ago that I wasn't going to go back because they always brought in authorities from out of town. These authorities would then tell us what we needed to do to get it right. And I was up to here with being fixed. I am who I am. I am what I am. So I didn't need a guilt trip provided by the Archdiocese of Louisville when all of us get together as priests. So I decided not to go for a while.

Well, three years have passed. A lot of things have happened in these past three years. So I felt the need to associate with the priests of the diocese. I was feeling a bit on the outside and isolated. So I called a priest friend and asked him to travel with me. I drove my car, in case I wanted to leave early. I had my exit plan.

It was good to see St. Meinrad. It is a beautiful complex. I spent four years there so I am very familiar with it. Things went well the first evening. We had a delightful meal catching up with each other. The first real event was night prayer, or Vespers. All of us gathered with the monks and we shared prayer. That in itself was a moving experience, especially with all male voices in a church that echoes and lends itself to chanting. The prayer was conducted by the monks and was very well done. It sort of settled the group.

At some time that night, I began to take my usual inventory. "Oh, there's so and so." Over a period of years, we tend to categorize everybody. We tend to put them in little boxes. You probably do this too. But I soon went to my room and did some reading. It was nice. St. Meinrad has this grand set of bells that ring every fifteen minutes all through the night. I had forgotten that. But I managed to sleep and I was ready for the next day. After breakfast, we gathered for Mass.

Again, the liturgy was a wonderful experience. It took me to a higher level in my thought process. I realized that the thing we all had in common was the Eucharist. After we broke open the Word and listened to Sacred Scripture for that day and made our intentions, we moved to a large space around the altar. There we confected the Eucharist together. That made me realize that truly, the greatest gift that you and I have received to aid us on our spiritual journey is the Gift of the Eucharist.

All of these priests, gathered in this church, brought different things for the celebration. Just like each one of you brings different things for *this* celebration. And the thing that you bring is not sanctity, holiness, virtue, piety or anything like that. Leave that stuff home. Bring yourself. Bring your humanity. Bring your fears and joys. Bring your anxiety. Bring your resentments. Bring those things that you and I know so well. These are the elements and the gifts that we give to the celebrant and to the community to be accepted by God.

We bring the ordinary things of bread and wine to be changed into the Body and Blood of Christ. But we are not idle spectators when we come to experience the Eucharist. We are participants. Eucharist comes from a Greek word that means thanksgiving. So we come with a spirit of thanksgiving for the life that we have, where we are and what we are doing. But Eucharist is both a noun and a verb. We are well aware of the noun, which is the element of the sacrament—the bread and wine changed into the Body and Blood of Christ. We can see it. We can taste it. We can smell it. It has substance and density.

But there is another part of the Eucharist that we have to experience. And that is the verb—what we bring with us. It is the action that we perform together as a community around this altar.

And that is called Eucharist also. When we can bring all the stuff that we carry as human beings in our life, and some of the residue from the past or fear of the future, and when the priest offers up the wine and the bread and we project our own stuff, our package, our gift onto that paten and chalice, then we participate in a very profound way.

What we do is leave our stuff here on this altar, only to be changed, only to be repackaged, only to be lightened or redirected. We receive our gifts back at the end of the Sacrament of the Eucharist and we realize that they are a little lighter, or that they have changed, or in some cases, that they no longer exist. There is a transformation that goes on, not only in the bread and the wine, but also in our own lives.

I looked at all those priests there, from the middle section of Kentucky, and one from Cambodia, who is a minister of sign language from Louisville, Fr. Charlie Dittmeier. All of us brought different gifts. And the monks had their gifts there also. What I began to be aware of and to really appreciate again was something that wasn't new to me, but something that I had taken for granted. This was the opportunity to gather for prayer, for reflection, for the giving of our gifts, for receiving and for continuing on with life.

If you want another concept of Eucharist, try this one on. The priest who gave the homily for the Healing Service for those who were sick talked about his illness. A year ago at the Presbyteral Assembly he was anointed. He then went into surgery, a coma for 22 days, terrible pain, two heart attacks, and so on. He used to be very articulate and very dynamic. He has slowed down a lot. He told his story. At the end, he told us that he firmly believes that what sustained him on his journey through the illness were friends. These were the people who had been part of his life all along, his family and his friends. He felt that these people, and many others whom he didn't know, loved him back to health, as if they were all holding out their hands, supporting him as he went through this horrific illness. I liked that thought—"to be loved back to health."

That is what we do with the Eucharist. When we come together as a community, we are performing that verb of Eucharist by loving each other back to health. None of us can stand alone. Not one of us can get through life by ourselves. We need each other.

One time I tried to say Mass by myself. No one was here. I proclaimed the Word. I said, "Let us pray." No response. I tried to celebrate. But this is a dialogue. This is an exchange that you and I do. This is what makes it real. And in that process, we love each other back to health—spiritual health, emotional health, physical health.

And so today, we celebrate the Feast of this tremendous gift. So many times we take it for granted. This gift is so unique and so wonderful in our own Christian experience. And there are no strings attached to this gift. It is not a prize that we win for doing something. It all has to do with our disposition — our disposition to receive the Body and Blood of Christ. And no one can take that away from us.

The Eucharist is ours. It is a free gift to us from God, through Jesus Christ. It is all contingent upon our disposition, where we are, and how we can come forward and receive. In my mind, there is no one there to judge. Who am I to judge? Who am I to say that someone cannot or will not be able to come to Communion. I can't. And I don't know anyone in existence who can. That is how unique the gift is. This is what we celebrate today as we gather together.

I must tell you that I felt a bit like Rip Van Winkle later on that Tuesday afternoon. I was in my room after I had taken a walk. I thought, "Where have I been for the last three or four years, with these guys, with the Church, with my own spirituality, with my journey? It is as if, all of a sudden, I am coming out of a deep sleep. I am looking around and I like what I am seeing. I like it a lot.

At no time, in the experience of the Presbyteral Assembly, were we told to be fixed. No one told us that we had to do this or had to do that! The assembly was conducted by the priests themselves. The Archbishop was there as a spectator. He sat on the side and didn't say a word.

So, it was a busy week. I've got to tell you that, being in recovery now, I have signed up for next year.

No Need for Fig Leaves

Genesis 2:7-9; 3:1-7
Romans 5:12, 17-19
Matthew 4: 1-11

For us to appreciate scripture, it is important that we remember that scripture was first spoken, not written. The story of God's relationship with His creation was a spoken story that was repeated over the centuries. Then, it was written down. Whenever I read the Genesis story of Adam and Eve, I often think about crossroads in the desert, the great trade routes where people would be carrying spices and other precious commodities from one place to another. They would stop at an oasis for the night. They would feed their animals. They would find food and sit around and eat, drink and discuss things. They would look at the bright stars in the sky. They would ask themselves the question: "How did this whole thing get started?"

Then they would take the ordinary things that they were familiar with: man/woman, black/ white, good/evil and all the rest, and over a long period of time a story was woven out of these things that they had experienced. Interestingly enough, this was not unique to the Jewish customs or the Jewish traditions. If we go back and look at various civilizations that existed, we will find that they all had a similar story of a man and a woman in paradise. They had a God. They had a transgression of some sort. So evolved the story of Adam and Eve and what we call original sin.

Today, on the first Sunday of Lent, we begin our Lenten journey with this story. It is important for us to reflect on this story, especially with the two readings that accompany the Genesis account,

Paul's Letter to the Romans and the Gospel of Matthew.

So we look at the story of Adam and Eve, which we call, technically, a myth. Now you know that the proper definition of a myth is not something that somebody just simply made up. It is an attempt to understand. It is with that definition in mind that I am presenting this homily this morning. It is an attempt to understand something that is not clear at the onset.

We find that God created this magnificent garden called the Garden of Eden. He created his two prime creatures, his masterpieces, man and woman. He set them into this idyllic experience, where all of their needs were fulfilled. They wanted for nothing. They were absolutely happy. There is a figure that comes into the story, the snake. A snake has always been depicted as one who is sly, cunning and evil. A good definition for a temptation, actually.

Within them, this question began to rise: What would it be like if we took matters into our own hands? If we did something that we weren't supposed to do, what would happen? Maybe we would know more, or maybe as much as God. So the story says.

Well, we know that there was a transgression. Some scripture scholars say that immediately upon the transgression there was a surge that went through the human experience. That surge had two heads. One head is *blame*, because he blamed her for the apple, which, by the way, is not mentioned in Sacred Scripture. But he blamed her for being seductive enough to be able to seduce him into taking part of this fruit. The other head was *shame*.

You and I have all experienced blame and shame in the course of our lives. We've had someone point their finger and say: "Shame on you!" That has an effect on us. We feel small. We feel "less than." We feel like we are dirty. And then blame sounds like: "I know you did this." It is similar to guilt. We know we did this. We become aware of our own humanness and the reaction to our actions.

This blame and shame, then, carries us into what we know as a sin. A sin is when you and I make ourselves the center of God's universe. We think everything is going to swirl around us. Sin is a selfish act, difficult to define. We can define it in acts that we may or may not do, but when you come down to it, sin is a selfish act that we either participate in, or we do not participate in. It could be a sin of commission or omission.

When we find ourselves feeling less than, feeling shame, etc., then, according to the story, we start to cover ourselves. We hide ourselves. Scripture uses the idea of the "fig leaf" to cover ourselves and/or our actions. So many of us walk through life covered from head to toe with fig leaves, because we never had the opportunity to deal with shedding that type of thing, those selfish acts of ours that we call sin.

Now, we could stop here and say: "That's a nice story." It's traditional. Everybody knows the story of Adam and Eve. So what?

Then we go to the second reading and we see Paul writing to the Romans. He is trying to tell them something. He said, "Out of the person who brought death (referring to Adam) into the world, you also have Jesus Christ, who brought life." So there is the counterpart that has been set up. On one hand we lose, but on the other hand we gain. And generally, we gain more than we lose. We have been given a choice, a free will. You and I are not simply people who are identical to each other, physically, spiritually or emotionally. Each of us is unique in God's mind. Because we are unique, we have this opportunity, this ability to make a choice, to elect to continue caring for ourselves, or to give to others.

So what Paul says in the second reading is something that is sort of a foundation stone for our theology. That we, as the extended family of Christ, have a choice. And in making this choice, we don't have to suffer the consequences that Adam and Eve did, which was shame and blame. We have the opportunity to be able to give to others, to be the light. We can hand out, by the way we live our life, by the way we let go of our prejudices, the opportunity to bring life to others.

Then we say: "That's a nice story too!"

Finally, we have the Gospel for today. It is the temptations of Christ. It has always been sort of an interesting Gospel for me. Because we know who Jesus Christ is. We've read the book. We know how it's going to end. We could read through all of these temptations, but the devil is going to lose. And Jesus will win, because he is God. So we can sort of set that aside.

But when we think about our journey as Christian people,

we think about it, not from the standpoint of winning or losing, but as learning to be part of the greater dimension of God. We think about it as being instruments of God and recipients of God's grace. This is where we are challenged to strip ourselves of all that blocks us from God. We dispense with all of the fig leaves that we have covered ourselves with, to protect ourselves from being found out.

It is interesting that in the story of Genesis the word "I" is used only after the transgression. "I did this." "I was afraid." "I hide myself." "I was afraid of what you would do to me." "I was afraid of the punishment." Previous to that time, the word "I" was never used. It wasn't necessary, because there was no penalty for anything one did.

The same thing happens to us today. There is really no penalty for anything we do when we do it with the grace of God, and in the light of the presence of God. It is only when we do it in the darkness, in the secretness of our hearts, without the presence of God that we have to concern ourselves with how we are going to be found out. How the fig leaf is going to fit for this time.

In our journey into Lent this year, we might consider a theme that has to do with Adam and Eve, that mythical story that is as ancient as time. The theme is about the choices that we have: about how we cover ourselves up, and how burdensome it is to exist that way—when, on the other hand, we can exist in the freedom of God's love and light.

A little aside

The Vatican Museum has the world's best collection of ancient art, contemporary art, and a representation of all that mankind has been able to master and bring together as a source of creativity, beauty and history. For a long period of time, through the Middle Ages, any of the ancient statues that were brought in from Greece and Turkey, or Roman statues that were dug up from landfill, were all presented and put in pedestals along the corridors at the Museum.

Then there was a very conservative moment that came into

the Church, where the human body and the human form was not permitted to be depicted. One of the popes decided that all statues showing genitals were to be covered with plaster fig leaves. You go through this long exhibit and you see these big plaster fig leaves all over the place. But it was only for a period of time. They don't do that today.

This is a lesson in freedom, I think, a lesson in the appreciation of God's creation, which is also part of this Lenten journey. Every time I go to the Vatican Museum, I look at these silly white marble statues that are all covered up with plaster. It reminds me that life is just simply a big circle. It keeps going round and round. God must look down here and say: "Will they never learn?"

The Power of Forgiveness

John 14: 1-12

In an attempt to reassure his disciples, Jesus said, "Do not let your hearts be troubled. Have faith in God and faith in me." Then he makes a statement that the disciples begin to question. He says, "In my Father's house there are many dwelling places and I have prepared a place for you. I will come back to take you with me. Where I am you will also be."

The disciples liked this idea. They liked it a lot. It meant that there was going to be a continued relationship with this charismatic leader, Jesus, whom they were just getting to know. Then, Jesus makes the statement: "I am the Way and the Truth and the Life." Thomas asks, "What do you mean by that statement?" Jesus, in a true rabbinic response, simply makes the statement again. Thomas said, "We don't know where you are going. How can we know the Way?"

He continues the conversation with the disciples. Philip says, "We don't know much about you. We don't understand what you are talking about." Jesus looks at him and he tries to explain who he is, who his Father is, and what his whole mission is about.

Actually, when I read that Gospel, I think of myself as part Thomas and part Philip. I like to ask the same question that you might want to ask: "Where are we going? How can we find the Way?" There is still a lot we don't know about the whole mystery of God, the whole mystery of salvation, the whole mystery of spirituality. Suffice it to say that the key to the answers lies in this phrase: *I am the Way and the Truth and the Life.*

The Way: what does that mean? Well I suppose that every one of us, at the knee of our parents, began to learn what it means to follow the Way. We were told things like "Play with your friends." "Share your toys." "Don't fight." "Tell the truth." "Be sorry." I doubt if there is any one in this church this morning who has not had that litany repeated over and over to them. And you are repeating it to your children. My friends, therein lies the foundation stone for the Way.

It is a way of acting. It is a way of relating to each other. It is a way of relating to our community and to our world. That is the way that you and I, as Christian people, are to react to each other. We are to share, to look out for, to express love, to beg forgiveness and to accept forgiveness. Yet, it is so difficult to do, isn't it?

A couple of weeks ago, I was in Chicago with a couple of priests and had the good fortune of seeing an Off-Broadway Show. It was entitled *Sin: The Deposition of a Cardinal.* It is a play that is based on the public deposition of Cardinal Law, in Boston. It was written in the last two years about the scandal in the Church. I went to see the play with a little hesitancy, yet with curiosity. It was played in what they call the "black box." It was just simply a black room with a stage and no scenery. There were two tables. One was for the people taking the deposition, and one for the cardinal and his attorney.

As the depositions began, they addressed the cardinal. They asked him who he was and what he was about. They asked about his history. Then they began to ask pointed questions as to how he dealt with priests who were inappropriately acting out in his archdiocese. Over and over again he said, "Well, I delegated that to so and so." Or "I had some other bishop take care of that case," etc. As the story began to unfold, you began to see that this man could not respond to his people in a very simple way, by saying "I am sorry for my inability to take care of this situation."

There was an intermission and then the play continued. Another set of witnesses came forward, along with another set of attorneys. They had letters and documents and all the rest. But the cardinal could still not come to the point of saying "I'm sorry." The play ended with all of the actors walking off of the stage. A light focused down on the cardinal, seated at the table, realizing that the only avenue he had left to follow was that of resignation. And so we saw, at the end of the play, a very sober, somber audience. I think each one of us in the theater that night was saying, "Wouldn't it have been wonderful if he would have said he was sorry?"

You and I are forgiving people. And God knows I have made mistakes in my ministry. Yet, when I bring it to the parish or you hear about my mistake, I experience a loving forgiveness. Then we go on about our business. That is the way it should be in all of our relationships. Outside of the phrase "I love you," the other important phrase that you and I have learned is "I'm sorry." When two people can express sorrow and forgiveness, then there is a deeper bond that develops. I facetiously, but sometimes seriously, wish that every couple that I marry have the opportunity to have a fight or disagreement, so that they can make up. So that they can say to each other, "I'm sorry. I made a mistake."

Many times we hesitate to admit a fault because we think it implies weakness. That is so erroneous. What it really implies is strength, strength to be aware of the process that we are all in. We find that we are not all perfect and that we don't have to be perfect. We find that we can celebrate our humanness, and we can be patient with each other. Then we find life. We find the freedom to celebrate the experience of living. I think that is what Jesus was saying. We need not have our hearts troubled. We don't have to worry about what the guy sitting next to us is going to think. All we have to do is be truthful and say "I'm sorry."

Let me close the homily with a modern parable. A modern parable is one of my human experiences. A couple of years ago I was having a bad day. Things were not going the way I thought they should. Everybody was busy in the rectory. The phone was ringing off the hook. Finally, I picked the phone up. And I didn't say, "Good Morning, this is St. Frances of Rome. May I help you?" Instead, I said, "HELLO." The person said, "Is so-and-so there?" "NO!" Then she said, "Perhaps I ought to call back." "THAT'S A GOOD IDEA!" Then she hung up!

The minute I did that I knew in my very bones that I should have never acted that way. I needed to find out who it was who called and I needed to go and apologize. So I went to the Identi-caller. It was dead! The battery was dead and I had no name. So I thought, "What am I going to do?" I was sorry that I had made such a stupid response on the phone, but I had no way to make amends.

Well the week passed and I got into a better mood. Things were looking much better for the most part. It just so happened that it was a beautiful Sunday morning like this. I was walking over from the Rectory to the Church to say Mass, and I ran into a parishioner who is always in a good mood. She said, "How are you?" I said, "I'm fine. How are you?" She answered, "I'm fine. I've got a gift for you." And I said, "Really?" Then she said, "It's an answering machine." I said, "Really! But we have one!" She replied, "Well, maybe you need another one!"

Then I said, "Why do you want to give us an answering machine?" "Well," she said, "earlier this week I called over to the Rectory, and I got this grouchy old man on the phone." And I thought, Oh my! Get the nails! So I said rather sheepishly, "Oh? When was that? What day did you call? What time was it?" I was treading water at this point, because I knew I was being confronted by a very gentle person, whom I could have offended by my response on the phone.

So I admitted, "You've got me! I'm so glad to find the person I was so rude to. I felt very bad about it and I am sorry. Will you forgive me?" She gave me a big hug and said, "Yes, of course. We all have those days, don't we?" And I said, "Yeah. I try not to have too many of them." She replied, "Seriously, if you need help answering the phone, let me know. I'll be glad to help anytime."

Now, think about this. Think about all of her reactions when she put that phone down after talking to that grouchy old man. She could have said, "I'll never darken the doors of that place again!" Or she might have said, "That man is out of his mind!" She could have said all kinds of things. But she didn't. She kept it to herself. (I think!) She knew that she was going to see me and that we would have that opportunity for a dialogue. Out of that dialogue the opportunity to say "I'm sorry" was given, the gift of forgiveness was given and the bond of love made closer.

What does it all mean? The more we think about it, the

more we realize that, indeed, Jesus is the Way, the Truth, and the Life. The "Way" is how we live out our lives. When we adopt Jesus' formula for successful living, which is love and forgiveness, then we begin to understand what "Truth" is. Truth is respect. Truth is accepting life on life's terms. Truth is letting God walk with us through life. And as a result of that, then we understand what "Life" really is. Life is a passage. It is a passage from one existence to another.

I think Jesus was giving us some hints about our human attempts to live life. If we try to live our human life with love and forgiveness, we won't have to worry about what is going to happen when "I come back to take you with me."

In the Process of Becoming

2 Timothy 4: 6-8, 17-18
Matthew 16: 13-19

I have an acquaintance who has the most amazing imagination. I've known this individual for a long time. Since I first met him, each time I went to his home, I noticed that various objects would show up that he had collected. There was an old painting of a gentleman in a military uniform hanging over the fireplace. I asked him who it was. He said, "Oh, that is great, great Uncle John. He fought in the Indian War." There was a photo of a woman on a table and I asked about her. "Well, that was my great Aunt. She lived during the Revolution."

Every time I went to his place, I saw something new and there was always a story about it. I was just amazed with his whole collection of very interesting family members in paintings, photos, and other forms of art. After several years, I discovered that all of this was part of his imagination. None of this was real. It was stuff that he had bought at a sale or at an auction. He created a fictitious world to live in. I couldn't believe it! Yet, he knew what he was doing. He told me, "None of this stuff is real!"

I have never forgotten that experience. I think that he is still doing this. He is still living in this other world of creation. He is still in this relationship with these people who are part of his imagination.

Today, we have a relationship with Peter and Paul that we are celebrating. I can guarantee that it is not a figment of our imagination. Quite the contrary! Peter and Paul were very real individuals. Peter, of course, was an apostle and is spoken of in all four gospels. Paul's works are recorded in the Acts of the Apostles. They were both key figures in the development of the Church.

In Greece, Spain, Italy, Turkey and all around the Mediterranean, there are great celebrations today on this Feast day. Don't make the mistake of thinking that Peter and Paul died on this particular day. This day was chosen as their feast because it was supposed to be the day of the birth of Romulus and Remus and the foundation of Rome. So the Church took that pagan celebration, and as they did in those days, affixed the Christian meaning to the special day.

It is refreshing to you and to me to take time to revisit these two great men. They were as different as they could possibly be. Peter was an ordinary fisherman, married, who lived in Capernaum. He had a little fishing business apparently, and was looking for something more, something he perceived that Jesus had.

I've long had the impression that it was his way out, a way out of the fishing business, a way out of being ordinary. I think we would all agree that Peter had a pretty big ego. He was always the first to make a statement. He was always the first to walk on water, and yet, failed, because he feared. He didn't trust Jesus. He was the one who said, "I will never, never let you wash my feet." But Jesus replied, "If you don't let me wash your feet, you will never be part of the Kingdom of God." So Peter was torn. He needed to be in control, and yet he was frightened.

Even after the Resurrection, Peter had a difficult time. The others looked to him for leadership and he assumed that role. But the wonderful thing about Peter is that we can trace the evolution of the change in his personality.

We can do the same thing with Paul. Paul was rugged. He was literate. He was a Roman, but he was also Jewish. He was out to make his mark in the world. He had a garrison of soldiers who were out to control the uprising of Christians, or the People of the Way, as they were called in those days. It was in the process of going to Damascus that he was struck blind. Then he came to the realization that what he was doing was something that was not going to bring him that which he was looking for—a sense of well-being, peace and the ultimate spiritual life.

So as we reflect on these two individuals, we can also reflect on our own lives. We can see that we are in the process of becoming. We haven't arrived. We'll never arrive. But we have the facility to change or to be changed, or we are forced to change our direction in life many times over. It has always been my experience that our reasons for starting on a particular path change over a period of time and we never reach that particular goal. There is always something that comes in and changes the course.

I was on a sabbatical several years ago and I was asked to write the story of my journey. I wrote some paragraphs on the reason why I decided to go to the seminary. And the reason I decided to go to the seminary was not the reason why I became a priest. Over a period of time, those reasons became very mundane. They had no value or meaning to them.

It is the same with entering into a marriage. The reason for entering into a marriage can be valid, but it will still change over a period of time. The reason why a couple stays married, the reason why they choose to grow in love, the reason why they allow themselves to celebrate the Sacrament of marriage will change also. We are always in the process of change.

In the second reading, Paul makes a wonderful statement. He says something like, "I have run the race. I have earned merit and crown. I am now ready for the next episode in living." It is a great consolation when you and I can say that. That we have lived our lives. That we have, hopefully, little or no regret. We have found life to be a journey, not fixed, not carved in stone but very fluid. That makes it possible for us to participate in what we discover in the process of living.

At the 9 a.m. Mass, we recognized the oldest woman in our parish, Hattie Brown. She is 100 today. She is a remarkable woman. She is an inspiration to me and to others. She and her husband came to this community to teach caning at the Blind School. I had a chair last year that needed a new seat in it, so I took it over to her and asked if she could re-cane it for me. She said, "Sure. I'll have it done in a couple of days." And she had it done before that. One of her hobbies is to play solitaire on the computer. At 100! Another one is to go to the casino. That's okay too. She is a woman who enjoys living and she has a great zest for living. She has "run the race."

Her house is decorated with her memorabilia. But I can tell you this: every picture, every embroidery piece, every object in that house is real. It is not a figment of her imagination. It is a demonstration of where she has been. On occasion when I have been to see her, I'll point to a picture and say, "Tell me about that." "Oh," she says, "that's when I went on a trip to Yellowstone." She has a story for each object.

I think the remarkable thing about Hattie is that she has allowed herself to be flexible. Many of you have done this also. That's what I think we celebrate today with the Feast of Peter and Paul. They came from one place and were able to move on—one a fisherman and one who was out to destroy the Christians. Paul is now known as the Apostle of the Gentiles who brought the Christian message to the entire Roman Empire. And, of course, Peter is known as the Apostle of the Jewish people.

That is our charge. That is our calling. To be flexible and available. As Paul says, "To let the grace of God work in our hearts as we continue our journey." As Hattie has given so freely of the many gifts she has acquired over the years, so we are challenged by her presence, to give freely what we have to give. We are challenged to continue the process that we have already begun.

Just Be the Passenger

Matthew 2:1-12

One of the traditions of Christianity has always been the story of the Magi, or Three Kings. There are a lot of myths and interpretations about these three individuals. They represent us. The Feast of the Epiphany really is the manifestation of Jesus to us Gentiles. Among the stories that are told, there is one that is a favorite of mine. I want to share it with you this morning.

The three magi, Caspar, Balthazar, and Melchior were not of the same age. The oldest one was Melchior. He was a senior citizen. Balthazar was middle-aged, energetic and still very interested in life and what was going on in life. Caspar was the youngest of the kings, or astrologers, and he was excited about what was going to happen next.

As the story goes, they finally reached Bethlehem. So, being the eldest, Melchior went in first to visit the family. But to his surprise, when he reached the interior of the house there was no family there. The only one who was there was an old man. So Melchior and this old man started talking about memories: about how things used to be, about the way it was when they were on the throne or when they were in control. They also spoke of gratitude: how grateful they were to have the opportunity to continue life, even with its aches and pains. So after the visit, Melchior left.

Then the middle-aged king came in and he found no family either. When he walked in, he saw a teacher. This teacher started talking to him about the various issues of life: about responsibility, about learning, about leadership. They spent quite a bit of time in conversation. Finally, Balthazar left the house.

Then Caspar, the youngest, went in for his visit. He also found no child and no manger and no mother or father. What he found was a young philosopher. The young philosopher and he got into a conversation about reform, and about the things that can happen if only we put our minds to it. They talked about dreams. They talked about life.

The three kings then gathered outside and prepared their gifts. They took their gifts into the house and there they met Jesus, Mary and Joseph. They shared their gifts with them. They left, by another route, to continue their journey back home. It was only on that journey that they began to discuss what had happened to them when they went to visit the family in Bethlehem. They talked about how each was met by a different individual: an older man, a teacher and a young philosopher.

Then they discovered that the topics were a lot different. The basic topic of the old man and Melchior was that of integrity and wisdom: about how important it is to be honest and straightforward in life, and about the gift of wisdom that is given with age. Balthazar was surprised, because his conversation had to do with service and responsibility. He learned about the opportunity he had to meet others on the way of life and the responsibility he had to share with them, without wanting something in return.

Then, of course, the young man, Caspar, told them of his conversation. It had to do with identity, and with intimacy. He found great solace in being able to talk to this young philosopher, because both of them were looking for identity and for intimacy. They recognized the fear that is involved in intimacy.

So, the story of the three Magi has to do with God speaking to each one of us at the place we are in life, here and now, whether we are young, middle-aged or retired, where we have memories and gratitude to think about. God speaks to each one of us at that place in life where we find ourselves today. The things we bring with us this morning, our troubles and our frustrations and all of the other things that we may be carrying around as our burden, are really gifts. But they are gifts only if you and I can take these gifts and give them to God for safekeeping.

We don't bring with us, as I have said so many times before, righteousness, holiness and sanctity. We bring our human experience.

In the story of the Three Magi that I have related to you this morning, that is what they talked about—their human experience. They talked about where they have been or where they hope to go or what they are experiencing in life. And they are not alone, because God is with them.

I have a good friend who is a monk. He is a respected spiritual director. He is a bit gregarious. He is spiritual director of one of my friends, a couple of years older than I am. He told me about having a difficult time convincing one of his directees to see that God is really in charge when it comes to living life and that our task is to turn things over to God and let Him take care of us. Let God be God for us, just as God was being God for the three Magi. This monk said that his directee is always assuming responsibility. He loves control. He worries and he gets himself into a fit and then he calls his spiritual director and says, "This is what's happening to me and I've got to change this and I've got to change that." The spiritual director, the wise old monk says, "Leave it alone. Cool it. Let God take care of things for you." And this is the hardest thing in the world for this guy.

So recently, he was on his way to Indianapolis. He had his cell phone with him and he was just getting himself agitated. He was worried about this and about that and how it was going to work out. So he called up the monk. He was explaining all of this to the monk who then asked him, "Where are you right now?" The directee replied, "I have just passed Sellersburg and I am continuing on the road." The monk then said, "Pull over to the side of the road and stop the car." The man replied, "Are you serious?" The monk replied, "Yes." So he did, and then asked what he should do next. The director then told him to walk around to the other side and get in the passenger side. The directee did that and told him so. Then the director said, "Now stay there until you realize that God is the driver of that vehicle!"

The directee then said, "Oh, that's what you are trying to tell me?" The director said, "That's right. Let God drive the vehicle for you. Just be the passenger." The reply was, "That's the damnedest advice I've ever had in my life!"

But that is true. That is the message of Epiphany. The message is, "Let God be God."

I haven't made any resolutions this year. I'm not going to. I've decided that I've given up resolutions. I have broken every resolution I've ever made. But I'm going to try something new. What I'm going to try to do is to live one day at a time. And make that day the day where I can be kind to someone, where I can be more patient, where I can be less judgmental, where I can be honest, where I can take time for myself, where I can get some exercise, and so on.

So I suggest that we block our resolutions at the very beginning, because we usually make them entirely impossible to attain. But if we take each day, and sometimes each hour, and sometimes each minute, as the only time we have to be responsible, we can live our day in a successful, virtuous way. Anything that comes to us in that day can be seen as a gift or a challenge. In doing so, I think we find the grace we need to continue our journey. Whether it has to do with intimacy or integrity, whether it has to do with memories and gratitude, whether it has to do with new discoveries or what is around the corner: it really doesn't matter. God is speaking to each one of us, just simply the way we are and where we are in the journey of life.

Accepting Our Imperfections

Luke 24:35-48

The Gospel today is the last part of the gospel that relates the story of the journey to Emmaus. Remember, that is the story of two disciples who were confounded about what had happened in Jerusalem, i.e., about Jesus being arrested and put to death. They were despondent so they decided to move on to Emmaus. A stranger joined them during the walk. He walked along with them and asked them questions about why they were so upset. They replied, "You must be the only one in the territory who doesn't know what happened to Jesus of Nazareth." They continued along together and eventually they asked him to stop and break bread with them.

It was only in the breaking of the bread, as Scripture tells us, that Jesus appeared to them and they recognized him as the Christ. At this point, Jesus left them and they went back to where the other disciples were hiding in Jerusalem. They brought the message about seeing Christ. So in the portion of the gospel we have today, we find Jesus coming to this place. As he walks in, he gives his usual greeting, "Peace be to you." As we know, this peace has another meaning. It has the meaning of peace of the emotions, of spiritual dimension, of physical dimension, of the whole person. Jesus proves to them that he is indeed with them and that he is the Savior.

He speaks now of the gift of Easter. He speaks of the gift of the Resurrection. The gift of the Resurrection has to do with the forgiveness of all things. That forgiveness is ours if we embrace it. It is ours for the taking. As you and I live our lives, forgiveness is one of the things that we have to deal with.

But to forgive and to deal with forgiveness is another matter. Earlier this week I was talking to a couple who live in my neighborhood. They were talking about the difficulties in the neighborhood. The more they talked about these difficulties the more I realized that, "my gosh, we are going to have war here in the neighborhood!" Everybody is upset. It was over foolish things like: "kids are throwing rocks on the driveway," "she cut down those big trees last year and she hasn't removed the stumps yet, and I tried to recommend someone to remove her stumps and she got mad!"

Do you realize that we deal with this kind of stuff in our lives constantly? When you really pause and think about the things that make us get upset, they are usually trivial, incidental situations. But for whatever reason, we hold onto them. We hold on tenaciously because "this is our space," "this is my place," "this is my decision and it is going to be this way!" I think the whole issue has to do with control, but I'm not sure. Maybe some of you can speak with more authority on this than I can.

When we talk about forgiveness, the first issue has to do with being able to admit our imperfections before God. That's where we begin the process of forgiveness. If we think we are righteous pillars of all that is spiritual and holy before God, then we are never going to be able to admit our weaknesses. Let's face it. We are all imperfect. That is part and parcel of being human. But it is also one of the great assets that you and I have as human beings.

The Renew small group that I am part of has recently read a book entitled *The Spirituality of Imperfection*. It is a wonderful book. It gives the history of spirituality and the place of imperfections in our lives. It tells us that for 1500 years or so, up until the Reformation, all of the spiritual leaders of the Church stressed the ability to accept imperfection in our lives—that imperfections are the things we are able to present to God to be forgiven for. As I have said in other homilies, if we were all perfect beings, as we have been taught to strive for since the Reformation, then God would be out of a job. He would have nothing to do. Because God has come to forgive us and to save us, he allows us to be the people we are, imperfections and all.

One of the things that happened after the Reformation was

the whole concept of having to be perfect in the eyes of all people. So we were taught at a young age that imperfection was unacceptable and that only perfection was acceptable. The first key in dealing with forgiveness is being able to address ourselves as we really are. That includes the blame and the shame that has been part of our lives, not to hide it, but to embrace it. Once we can do that before our God, then we can accept it. We can accept the way we are and not the way we think we ought to be.

It is encouraging to learn that it's okay to have wrinkles and warts and habits that drive other people to distraction. That is simply the way we are.

The other element of forgiveness is to be able to share it with another individual. When we are able to share our imperfections with another individual, then we can see them clearly. We see them from another person's viewpoint. I remember some years ago that I had the opportunity to search out someone that I needed to talk to. And there was some criteria that I wanted this individual to have. I wanted this individual to be talented in his field of psychiatry. I wanted this individual to be of a religious persuasion other than Roman Catholic. The person I asked about finding such an individual wanted to know why I didn't want a Roman Catholic. I answered, "I know all the Catholic stuff. I need a frame of reference so he can make a judgment now and then. I'm looking for someone else's opinion to look at my situation."

Therein we have an exchange and find truth. If we only go to those people who always agree with us, we learn nothing. We need to have an outsider look at our situation and say, "You have nothing to worry about. You are forgiven. Be at peace."

The message of the Resurrection has to do with our ability to forgive and our ability to accept ourselves as we are, and with our ability to look for a very clear image of ourselves as we go through our spiritual journey. That is what I think Jesus meant when he came into the room where the disciples were gathered and said, "Peace be with you." He said a lot more than just those few words. It was a profound message that we struggle with even today. It is okay to be imperfect and it is okay to accept ourselves as we are. We are loved by God because we are that way. We can then forgive ourselves and be ready to forgive others.

That is what the Easter season is all about. It is about being able to understand who we are, where we are, and how we can love each other.

Legacy of John Paul II

John 20:19-31

The line in this morning's Gospel that reads, "Do you believe because you have seen, or do you believe because of your faith?" is a question so appropriate for us as we gather with the entire Christian World to celebrate the life of Pope John Paul II. It is so easy, as the Gospel tells us today, to have preconceived ideas about literally anything and everything. Whether we have experience as a reference, or whether we have hearsay as a reference, or whether it is just simply a conclusion that we have come to, we all have our own opinions on church, faith, hope, issues, people, things.

When we find ourselves in this position, we also realize that we are in a dangerous position. Because this is, many times, erroneous. We have a mistaken notion. Yet we build our life or our opinion or our faith on this mistaken notion. This happens to all of us.

One of the great volumes that I know about the history of the Catholic Church was written by a man named Will Durant. I think it was published in the 1950s. It was probably the most comprehensive history of the Roman Catholic Church up to that date and maybe even today. If you were to pick up the volumes of Will Durant's work on the Church, you would find out that, first of all, it is a human institution. We say this because we are human, because the one who has been elected as pope is human. There are human experiences that every century brings and we have to deal with them. That's why, when reading the history of the Church, it is not cut and dried. It is filled with all kinds of experiences, whether it is the development of nations, or the invasion of foreign armies or whatever it might be. It is rich in tradition and human experience.

There have been a lot of different experiences that you and I have had. One of the things that I think we often fail to realize is how vast the work of the Church is and what effect it has on the people of the world.

I first learned this many years ago when I went to Rome for the first time. There was a Brother who taught at St. X, named Brother Thomas More, the Disciplinarian in the 50s, who was in Rome. He was working at the headquarters of the Xaverian Brothers. I called him up and said that I was in Rome for a while and would like to have dinner with him. He agreed and we went to a little place and caught up with each other after a break of about 15 or 20 years. I said, "What are you doing here in Rome?" He said, "I have the best job going. I put together missionaries and civil engineers." I said, "Now explain that to me!"

He continued, "Well, you have a lot of Third World Countries with no infrastructure. There are civil engineers who can come in and build dams and set up irrigation and provide for the basic needs of the people. But they need someone who knows the language, who knows the history, who knows the culture of the land. The missionaries are responsible for these skills. So what we do with the U.N. is to put engineers and missionaries together, and we send these teams out into the Third World countries. The missionaries make sure that the scientists do not step on the traditions and ways of the people."

I was fascinated. I had never thought about how all of this works. I realized that this was just one small aspect of the great work of the Church. I realized that Rome has planned many ways for the Church to have an effect all over the world. The man whose life we celebrate this week, Pope John Paul II, was born in a Second World country. He was raised under the Communist influence. His mother died when he was eight years old. He was an orphan by 20. His brother was a doctor who also died. Yet, he was dedicated to his faith and his belief in God. He was also an athlete and an actor. He started an underground theater movement that spoke against Communism. He eventually went to the seminary—an underground seminary by the way.

When the Cardinal from Poland came to Rome 26 years ago to elect a new pope, he never returned to his homeland other than for a visit. What a change it was for everyone, and what a surprise, because he was the first non-Italian to be elected pope in centuries. John Paul brought his unique gifts and he shared those gifts with us in so many different ways. He is the most traveled man we have ever had in the papacy. He has touched the lives of more people than any other pope. Just the presence of this man is powerful. International leaders have sought out his company. When he was invited to a particular country he would agree to come, but he also told the committee that he would talk about the rights of the individual.

The bottom line of John Paul's theology had to do with the dignity and rights of each human being. That was his ministry. He went forward to meet, to greet, and to change. He had a profound effect on the people of Cuba. Before the Pope came to Cuba, the people used to sneak into the Catholic Church. After his visit, they stood up and walked in, not fearful any longer.

My closest experience with the Pope happened on my sabbatical in 1987. One of the things that all priests look forward to when we go to Rome is the opportunity to celebrate Liturgy with the Holy Father. Well, a group from Louisville came on Palm Sunday that year and had Holy Week with me and the rest of us in Rome. Then we took off that Easter and went traveling to Florence and on up to Venice and other cities. I met one of my colleagues from New York in Harry's Bar in Venice. He told me that he had word that our class had Mass with the Pope on Easter Monday and that we had missed it. I said, "Don't worry about that. We can make contact for another engagement with the Pope."

So we came back and every door we tried was closed! But I had a friend who was in the household of the Pope, Sister Alma LaBray. She was quite a gal. She was from the Philippines. I had tea with her one afternoon and I told her that I couldn't get in to have Mass with the Pope. She told me that it was certainly something I should do. So, that night the phone rang and it was the Secretary to the Pope. He said, "Would you and Fr. O'Connor be able to have Mass with the Holy Father tomorrow morning at 6 o'clock?" I said, "Oh, yes, yes."

So we went over to the small chapel they have been referring to on TV this morning, and he was sitting in his chair, praying. We vested and sat with other people, including political dignitaries and bishops. The Master of Ceremonies came over and said to Fr. O'Connor and me, "Would you both stand with the Pope, as deacon and sub-deacon?" So that's what we did. We stood on either side of John Paul for the liturgy. I was totally blown away with the experience. Then it came time for the sign of peace. The Pope turned to me and said in Latin, "Pax vobiscum." Now any of you who grew up when I did know that this meant "Peace be to you." And that the response is "Et cum spiritu tuo." Well, when he spoke to me, I was as blank as that wall! And all I could say was "And to you too!" He did sort of a double take and then he looked over at O'Connor, who by this time knew it all!

After Mass, we went back to take off our vestments. We went to the library to be greeted by the Pope. He was very kind. He said, "Where are you from?" "What do you do?" I said, "Your holiness, I am very embarrassed." And he replied, "Peace." Then he gave me a rosary.

John Paul II was that type of person. It was not unusual at all for his friends, even in his last months, to come from Poland and drop in on him. He had an open door policy for his classmates and his friends. He was a very human man.

I share these stories with you this morning, not because he was a pope, but because he, like you and me, received the gift of baptism and he used that gift with all his heart! That is what made it possible for the Pope to reach out and touch the lives of millions of people. That's what made it possible for him to be patient, to help secure the fall of Communism, and to do all the other things that he has done.

Some people have agreed with what John Paul has done. Some people haven't. But that's the risk you take when you are in the position of pope. The new pope we are going to receive in a few weeks will not satisfy everyone. It is impossible to satisfy the needs of everyone. All any pope can do is bring the gifts that he has been given through his baptism and share them with us.

That is what you and I need to do on our Christian journey.

We need to take our gifts of baptism and use those gifts to help us serve as the eyes, the ears, the mouth, the legs and the hands of Christ to others. That is our charge. When we do that, then change happens for the best. Peace comes. The work of God continues in our world.

Welcome to Our Table

John 10:1-10

Again, I welcome all of you here today as we celebrate a "rite of passage" for those who are going to make their First Communion. What is a rite of passage? It is a significant time or date in our lives when something happens. There used to be a lot of rites of passage. Unfortunately, that isn't the case today. The only two rites of passage that I can think of are when kids turn 16 and they get their driver's license, or when they turn 21 and they can drink alcohol! I can't think of any other times that are all that significant.

But in the tradition of our Church, we have a number of rites of passage. At the last Mass, a young couple whose wedding I had the privilege of witnessing, brought their first child to be baptized. We baptized William Brooks Jackson. So this little baby, who slept through his baptism, has been given to his parents and grandparents to shepherd him—to teach him his prayers, the right way to act, how to go to church, to be kind to others. He has begun his rite of passage as a Christian.

You children are about to enter into a rite of passage also. You are about to make your First Communion. I would think that the vast majority of the people in this church can probably remember when they made their First Communion. I remember when I received this sacrament. Interestingly enough, some things have changed since we made our First Communion. Your parents are your teachers. Your gold workbook has been worked on by you and your parents. It describes what First Communion is all about. I think they call it the "Golden Book."

Our parents weren't that involved when we made our First Communion. The sisters were involved, like Sister Mary Jo. But they taught all of us. We couldn't have a drink of water after midnight. Sister was so afraid we would break our fast. So they would tape up the water coolers at school. We were also told that when we received the Body and Blood of Jesus, we were not supposed to let our teeth touch the Host. I have never figured out what that really means! Personally, I don't think Jesus minds if our teeth touch him! But that was one of the rules.

Over a period of years, things have changed. But the basic idea of receiving Holy Communion hasn't changed. You are being invited to come to the table of the Lord, with all the rest of us. You are so welcome! We are excited about that.

What do you bring with you when you come to the table of the Lord? Well, you bring your stuff: the things you worry about, the things you don't feel good about, the things that are going on in your life, and you offer them to Jesus. Jesus takes these things and he blesses them. All the difficulties, the problems and the things that are bothering you, Jesus makes holy. Then he gives them back to you when you receive Holy Communion. He does this not only for you who are just beginning, but he does it for all of us.

During the Offertory, you notice that the wine and the bread are brought up, along with the Sunday collection. But the most important gift that you bring is where you are and what you are concerned about. Those are very valuable gifts. That's what it means to enter into a spiritual or holy experience with God. Now, sometimes, we simply just go to Communion. We don't really receive anything, because we haven't prepared ourselves to receive Holy Communion. We haven't taken the time to think about what is on our minds. It might be that what is on your mind is happiness. It might be great joy that you are offering at the table. This is important to give to God also, and to have it blessed. Or, it might be something that is worrying you. You also give that to be blessed.

In the Gospel today, we hear about Jesus being a shepherd. This is a good image for us to think about, especially you First Communicants. The role of a shepherd is to know his sheep and to care for them. You can go way back in the Old Testament, the oldest part of the Bible, up to the New Testament, and you will see that the image of the shepherd is used over and over again. What it really means is that we have a special relationship with this shepherd. And this relationship is love. God protects us from difficulties and dangers. He sees us through the problems of living, regardless of how old we are.

As you receive Holy Communion, you will begin to understand as time goes on, how valuable it is to be part of this Christian community. And how valuable it is for you to share what is in your hearts with this community. The people in this church can tell you what their First Communion was like. I would suggest that, during this liturgy, you adults try to remember what it was like. How did you feel when you first received the Body and Blood of Christ? Maybe you have a better appreciation now of how we all join around the table of the Lord, where we welcome these new members into full communion, and we share with them the same Body and Blood of Christ.

When we talk about the Body and Blood of Christ, we are really talking about the spiritual hunger that we have. All of us know what it means to feel sort of empty, where we have no place to turn, when we have a sense of uneasiness. We try to fill it up with all kinds of things. It might be a trip. It might be a movie. It might be a dinner. It might be a bigger bank account or a new relationship. But those things never work. The only thing that really fills up that empty spiritual spot is our relationship with God. And that is what we receive when we come to Communion.

To all of you, I wish you a Happy Anniversary of your First Communion. Think about it, and remember the words of the Psalmist David in the Old Testament: "Shepherd me and watch over me, O God, beyond my wants, beyond my fears, and bring me from death into life." The fullness of life comes when we participate in the Gift of the Lord in Holy Communion.

Congratulations to each of you, and remember that we are all praying for you as you receive your First Communion.

Lessons from the Baggage Department

1 Samuel 26:2, 7-13
1 Corinthians 15: 45-49
Luke 6:27-28

For the past seven weekends we have been celebrating, according to our liturgical calendar, Ordinary Time, the time between Epiphany and Lent. Wednesday of this week is Ash Wednesday, the beginning of Lent. During the period of these weeks, we have been introduced to the themes of Jesus' teachings. Most of these themes we have made part of our spiritual lives: to feed the hungry, to cure the sick, to give help to others. While we have these as part of our spiritual assets, today we are given the real challenge, the challenge that is probably the most difficult for all of us. And this has to do with forgiving others.

Jesus tells his disciples, "We have to love our enemies, and we have to forgive them." That is a very big order! All of us have such baggage, in varying degrees, whether it be from broken relationships, or from family squabbles, or from pain and hurt that we have received somewhere along the line. So, we sometimes say, "Was Jesus really serious when he said we had to forgive everyone?" After all, that is a pretty heavy task!

Yet, in the first reading, from Samuel, we find that an example was given. The reason why David didn't kill Saul when he had the opportunity was because he realized that Saul was the anointed one. He was anointed by God to carry God's message. He left his mark by taking his sword, but he did not take his life.

In the second reading, Paul suggests that in handling this

difficult experience of forgiveness, we have to remember that we were made in the image and likeness of God. This gives us a sense of dignity. Not only do we have this dignity individually, but we also have to give that dignity to everyone else. And that is a difficult thing to do! It means that we have to embrace, as one of God's anointed, Saddam Hussein, Hitler and terrorists. We have all kinds of challenges that we, as Christian people, have to assume because that is the sum and substance of being a Christian.

The Gospel today also challenges us in many different ways, not only in the element of forgiveness and love, but also in our everyday relationships with each other. It is a gospel that speaks to me personally.

I had been here at St. Frances of Rome about three years. Someone came to me, not a member of the parish, who was in need of financial aid. He had received a grant to go to college, and the grant had not come through. So the individual asked if I would lend him some money. I said I would and he told me he would pay the money back at the end of the month. So I lent him the money, and sure enough, I got the payment at the end of the month.

A couple of months later, the person came and said his grant had not been received for this segment, and could he borrow the money again. I said "Sure" and gave him the money. He paid it back by the end of the month. This went on for three times. The fourth time I lent him the money, it was not repaid by the end of the month. It was not repaid by the end of six months. I wondered what had happened. In good faith I had lent him the money, and up until now, it had been returned in good faith. As the months went on, I began to drive by his house, wondering what had happened. I left a message on his phone. It got to the point where it was really getting to me. It was eating me up! I began to obsess about it. "How could he do this to me after all I had done for him?"

I was a member of a priests' support group at the time, and so I brought the issue to them. I told them that the money had not been returned and I was angry about it. You know what their response was? They laughed! They just laughed. I said, "What's wrong with you all?" They replied, "Don't you realize that when you lend something to someone, you give it as a gift?" I said, "Where did you get that idea!" They said, "It's in Luke's Gospel!" So I can stand here today and tell you that 12 years ago, I learned something in the Gospel of Luke that I wasn't practicing!

The point is that you and I do not have the luxury of being able to carry around resentment, anger or frustration of that type. In effect, it will eat us alive. It becomes our issue. The resentments fill us up. We cope with that in varying ways. One of the many techniques is simply to have the great wall fall and say, "That person does not exist. He is totally out of my life forever." Or we can stew and we can ruminate and we can go by the house and see if the light is on. We can leave messages on the phone. We do ourselves in.

Every one of you, sitting here today, is no different from me, or I from you. We've all been there. We all have those resentments. We all have those angers. We all have those issues. And we are so right! We did the right thing for the individual!

And then my classmates introduced me to the Gospel of Luke, where he says: "Give without receiving." That was a significant breakthrough for me.

We have, this week, the opening of the movie, *The Passion*, by Mel Gibson. There has been a lot of comment about the movie. I have not seen it. I will, in time. But I am sure there is only one line in that movie that is the center of Jesus' message. It is the line that you and I need to remember today, while we are talking about anger and forgiveness and love and all the rest. It is when Jesus looked up to the heavens and he said, "Forgive them, Lord, for they do not know what they are doing." That sums it all up, right there. Who did Jesus say that to? Was it Pilate, who was a weak leader and bent to the crowd? Herod, who hated him? The soldiers, who nailed him to the cross? The people, who incited the rebellion? Who did Jesus have in mind when he said "Forgive them?"

Jesus had you and me in mind. He had all of God's creation, because within that moment, we became the anointed ones. God's anointing comes to us through Baptism and through the practice of our faith. When we are challenged to go ahead and forgive someone, not for their sake, but for ours, who benefits from this act of forgiveness? We do. We have to make amends and we have to say "That's all right." If that person accepts our forgiveness, so much the better. And if they don't, it is still all right. We have freed ourselves from the burden of such things as hate and anger and all that goes along with that. So, today, we come to the real kernel of Jesus' teaching: our need to forgive. It is difficult, but possible, and not always immediately. Sometimes it takes a lifetime to be able to get into the spirit of true forgiveness, but we have to be on the way to that end. We have to be in the process of doing it. And we have to be careful that we have a true perception of what is happening. This is because, from our standpoint, events are often going to be colored, clouded and possibly erroneous, to a great degree.

Let me tell you how my story ended. A year later, I received, unexpectedly, an envelope in the mail. It was a letter from the person I had lent the money to. He explained that, first of all, he was very embarrassed, but that he had fallen on some hard times. He wrote that he had appreciated the opportunity to have borrowed the money. He sent back, not the amount I had given him, but twice that amount. And all my ruminating, all my angst disappeared. And I can share it with you today. I don't have to carry that baggage anymore.

But I have other baggage that is still in storage! Yet, we go on, don't we? We continue our journey. But we free ourselves of that which keeps us from really being able to live out the message of Jesus.

The extra money became the seed money for a special program that has been in place here at St. Frances of Rome for many years. At times there are children in our parish who have need of special education and their families can't afford it. It has been the custom of our parish to provide that money.

I tell you today that I have learned a couple of things. I have learned that you give without expecting something in return. I have also learned the pain of misjudging others. How grateful I am for Jesus' words, "Forgive them, for they know not what they do."

The Ministry of Hospitality

Genesis 18:1-10
Luke 10:38-42

One of the great virtues of the Old and New Testaments that is repeated many times, just as in the first and third readings today, is that of hospitality. Abraham sees three strangers coming down the road and he looks upon them as if they can bring him a blessing. So he extends to them lodging, food, rest, shade and all that he and Sarah could put together in order to give them a warm welcome. We find this in various places in the Old Testament. Today, we have it in the New Testament with the story of Martha and Mary, who are the sisters of Lazarus.

This story follows on the gospel of last week, which was the story of the Good Samaritan. If you remember, we ended the discussion last week pondering over "Who is my neighbor?" Immediately, Luke picks up with the story of Martha and Mary, saying that everyone is our neighbor. I also suggested last week that it is important for us to know the manner and the customs of the time in which these particular episodes were set. So, as a bit of a background for today's gospel, you have to remember that Martha and Mary lived in a small town. It was five miles from Jerusalem, certainly a walkable distance.

Martha, Mary and Lazarus were unlike all the other friends of Jesus. They weren't like Jesus' disciples, people who followed him because they thought he could do something for them. They weren't like his apostles, who were being taught and trained in ministry. Martha, Mary and Lazarus were intimate friends of Jesus.

They were his family. They were his closest friends. He knew that he could simply show up at any time and chill out, as we would say.

In another passage of scripture, we know that Lazarus died and Jesus did not show up for three days. This was certainly out of character for Jesus. Mary sat quietly, crying. But Martha met Jesus on the road and she did not say the normal greeting like "It is so nice to see you," but she let him have it. She spewed forth her pain and her hurt with "Where were you when we needed you? If you would have been here, Lazarus would still be alive." That is the type of person Martha was. She was outgoing. She could organize any event that needed to be celebrated. She was always the first to the door. She was always speaking her mind. She was an aggressive woman. In contrast, her sister Mary was quiet. She was meditative. She enjoyed quiet conversation with Jesus.

In the scene that Luke gives us today, there are a few problems. First of all, we need to understand that Jesus didn't come by himself. He brought *the boys*. He always traveled with the apostles. So, since Martha knew Jesus was coming with his friends, she knew she had to prepare for 14 or 15 people. Second, it was the custom at that time in the area that all of the men would sit at the table first and be fed. The women waited on the men until they were finished. Then the men went outside and the ladies ate the leftovers. (After I gave this part of the sermon last night, it was suggested by someone that if she were Martha, and Jesus announced that he was bringing the boys with him, she would have suggested that Jesus stop by the closest delicatessen and bring his own food! But that wasn't the custom of the day.)

So the issue was about how Martha was going to feed all of these people. She had dealt with situations like this many times; she was certainly a woman of hospitality. On the other hand, there was the problem of Mary. Mary was doing something that was certainly out of character as well. Usually it was a pupil or a young man who would sit at the feet of the Teacher. But this time, it is Mary who is there in quiet dialogue with Jesus.

So we have two issues here that are sort of between the lines, if you will. At some point Martha comes into the room where Jesus and Mary are and says to Jesus, "Tell Mary to come and help me!" Jesus makes this reply, not meant to be a putdown to Martha, "Mary has chosen the better part, and she won't be deprived of it."

It seems to me that there is a bit of Martha and a bit of Mary in each one of us. We have these extremes in our personalities. We can become so involved in our work and in our activities and the things that we *have* to do, that we miss the moment of intimacy with God, with ourselves and with others. On the other hand, we can become so involved with reflection and meditation and intimacy with God or others that everything else sort of falls into chaos. These are the two extremes we have to deal with today.

There is a priest in the diocese that I have known for 50 years. He was ordained seven years before I was. Ever since I have known him, he has been talking about how hectic things are. How hectic theology was, how hectic his first appointment was, all the way up to today, where he recently stood up at the Presbyteral Assembly and talked about how hectic retirement is! So for some years I have been calling him Fr. Hectic. I know that he is always going to be living in turmoil. You know as well as I that there are people who walk through life carrying more than they can possibly handle because there is some emotional payoff. The payoff is "Gosh, look how hard you work!" Or, it is a way of staying away from intimacy: "Sorry, dear, can't do it. I've got to work." "Can't take care of the kids tonight. I've got to work." "Can't go to church on Sunday. I've got to work." There is a payoff for the person who lives a hectic life.

I think there is a payoff, too, when we don't do anything. When we leave it up to somebody else. When we simply become inert. And we can easily do this too, can't we?

Somewhere, I think we have to find a balance in life between these two biblical characters of Mary, who sits at the foot of Jesus, and Martha, who is stirring and rattling those pots and pans in the kitchen because all those guys have shown up for a meal. If we take it out of the biblical context and apply it to our own lives, it becomes somewhat of a challenge for us to look at life and to live life without becoming totally worn out, or losing our sense of relationship with each other.

This past week, I had a call from a friend, and he said, "What are you doing tonight?" I said, "I don't have any plans for tonight." He said, "Great. Why don't you come with my wife and me and maybe a couple of other friends. We are just going to get together."

I replied, "What is the occasion?" He said, "It's our date night." (I might tell you that they have four kids, all under about eight years.) "We decided some time ago that we need a night, once or twice a month, where the two of us can simply get together, either by ourselves or with friends, and just do something for ourselves." So I said, "That sounds like a great idea." We got together, met at the appropriate place, and we ended up at Slugger Field. It was the first time I had ever been to Slugger Field. We walked around, saw people we knew, sat down and enjoyed the game, and had a bratwurst and a drink. It was really nice.

I asked my friend, "How long have you been doing these date nights?" He said, "Oh, for about a year. And it really pays off. It gives us the opportunity to get away and to rediscover ourselves and each other. We'll have dinner together or we'll go back to the places we went to when we were dating. It is enriching. It is life-giving." And you know, it is giving them a sense of priority and a focus in their lives. It is a way to eliminate this concept of having to be busy at the marketplace or of being detached. I thought to myself that this couple really had something going for them, and that these four children are going to reap the benefits. They are going to learn the lesson that their parents are demonstrating with a date night.

So this morning, as you and I gather and ponder this passage, there is a lot to think about in regard to Martha and Mary. It is about hospitality and serving others, about the place of prayer in our lives, about how we can retain intimate relationships with God, with ourselves and with others. On the other hand, it is about the mistaken notion of being in a hectic state of mind.

I can guarantee you this: nobody in this diocese who knows me will ever call me "Father Hectic." It just ain't in the books! I learned a long time ago that there is no future for me to be in a hectic state of mind. How about you?

Dealing with the Human Dimension

Exodus 16:2-4, 12-15
Ephesians 4:17, 20-24
John 6:24-35

"Do not live, as the pagans do, in the futility of your mind." These words are taken from the second reading today. The futility of our minds: what an interesting statement. Human nature is indeed a curious and exasperating dimension of life. Whether we realize it or not, we find ourselves carrying around a lot of ideas that might have originated in our youth, which we still have in our emotional kitbags, and we rarely have the opportunity to deal with them.

It is important, however, that we deal with it all. Otherwise, we are like the Israelites in the first reading, who were complaining about the fact that they were under bondage in Egypt. So they got out of Egypt only to find themselves wandering in the desert with Moses and this caused them to complain about the fact that they didn't have any food. We've always got that opportunity to complain, complain and complain! We say that life is just not the way we want it to be. Or that we have been dealt a bad hand in the great game of life.

Human nature is simply human nature and we need to deal with it. This past week, I had the opportunity to attend a class reunion in New York. One afternoon I gave myself some time to visit museums. I went to the Whitney Museum. I had read the scriptures for today before I went on my trip, so when I got off the elevator of this museum and walked into the exhibit I just stopped in my tracks! The exhibit had to do with human nature. It had to do with my heroes of the past.

When I entered the exhibit, I saw all of the characters of the comic books that I had collected as a boy. One of my passions as a young kid was to have the biggest collection of comic books in St. Matthews. At the exhibit, I found, to my amazement, mannequins. There was Captain Marvel, Superman, the Jolly Green Giant and Wonder Lady. Superman greeted me, but he was there on a walker. He had a very bad toupee on the top of his head. I looked over at Wonder Lady and she had grown old too. She was skinny, her knees were together, she was no longer endowed as I had remembered, and she was standing next to Captain Marvel, who was on a gurney. There, in front of all of them, was the Jolly Green Giant. He appeared old and wrinkled, sitting in his chair, staring at the tube, green as he could be, still in his costume.

I thought to myself: "What has happened to all my heroes? They are all gone. They are as old as I am, if not older." Did you ever think of all those people getting old? No. Nancy is still young. Blondie and Dagwood haven't aged. But my heroes have.

It is part of the process, isn't it? If we don't have control of the process, then what do we do? We try to gain control and we do that by complaining. By blaming. By saying, "What is wrong with that person?" "Can't they see that the light is green?" "Why don't they signal when they turn in front of me?" "Why does it take so long for the waiter to bring me the bill?" "Why doesn't the doctor have a direct line so I can talk to him?" This is all part of human nature.

In Paul's letter, we have this wonderful line, "Don't live life as the pagans do, in the futility of the mind." The writer is challenging us to look beyond the mind to the Spirit. If we look into the Spirit and we allow God to be part of our life, and we enter into what we call human nature, then we find that life takes on a completely different dimension. We can, in effect, let our heroes grow up. We can allow ourselves to deal with our infirmities or our frustrations or our difficulties in the light of faith and in the light of process. We can do this, rather than always grasping for perfection as the Gentiles did in the second reading.

There is no such thing as perfection. There is absolutely no such thing as perfection! What really exists is process. And this means that we are constantly in the form of change. And, as I discovered so abruptly when I looked at those heroes of the past, there is change in my life also. I immediately gave up the whole need or desire to have the largest comic book collection in St. Matthews. Because that's not where it is.

Where it is, and what I think we are really looking for in life, is found in the gospel today. Jesus knew human nature so well. He knew what made those old people tick. So he confronted them. He said, "So did you come over from Capernaum just because I gave you something to eat? You want another free meal?" Then Jesus said, "That isn't where it is!" The people replied, "Give us a sign and we will believe in you."

"I'm not going to give you a sign. You don't need a sign. Because if I give you one sign you will ask for another one, then another, and another." We're back to human nature again.

If we live our life by the Spirit, the Spirit gives us all that we need to sustain ourselves on a daily basis. When joy comes, we can celebrate joy. When patience is demanded, we can celebrate patience. When we find ourselves angry, we can deal with anger. But that only happens when we are able to let things go and not have the need to control all that is around us.

It is so easy to complain, isn't it? I think complaining is somehow connected with fear. To always complain about something or someone or some situation has to do with the lack of control that we think we should have. It could be in the family, the business place, the Church, the government or whatever. We need to realize that control is not what we are really after. Freedom is what we are after. Then we can allow things simply to pass.

A little side comment: at the 9 o'clock Mass I was giving this homily. There was a gentleman sitting right there and when I mentioned the bit about not giving a turn signal, he broke up. So I suggested, "Let it go!" Then his wife elbowed him and said, "I've been telling you that for years!"

The message today, then, my friends, is that we are *human* beings, not *perfect* beings. Our frustrations need not be spilled forward. We don't need to live in the futility of our minds, where we have all of these things put in their proper places, and where we are dealing with them in the most remarkable way we possibly could. What we have to do is move ahead, as Jesus is trying to tell the people who have come and searched him out, "Don't be looking for signs, just be open to the Spirit." When you and I are open to the Spirit, then life takes on an entirely different dimension. And we are able to enjoy it.

And if by chance, I can find the article with pictures of the exhibit of our "old" heroes on the Internet, I will print it in the bulletin next week.

Where Have *We* Laid Jesus?

John 20: 1-9

I read in the paper this morning that Bob Russell had a full house yesterday. Well, let me tell you: he's got nothing on us! I think there are more people here now than at the 9 o'clock Mass this morning. And there was a good crowd last night at the Vigil. So to all of you: Welcome, and choicest blessings on this Easter.

For a moment, let's go back to Sacred Scripture and let's look for the similarities and the differences between the four accounts of the Resurrection found in our Gospels. They were all different. Of course, we realize that they were presented to different people at different times over the first seventy-five years of the Christian religion. But when we reflect on each of these particular gospels, we find that they have one thing in common. The one thing they have in common is disbelief and the need for discovery.

One of the gospels speaks of the women getting up early in the morning, taking the spices and going to the tomb to anoint the corpse of Jesus. When they arrived, they discovered that he wasn't there. Another gospel tells us that Mary Magdalene went to visit the tomb. She was very distraught because she couldn't find him. He wasn't there. Then she saw someone in the garden. She went to the garden and she said: "Where have you laid him? I need to find him." She recognized after she asked the question that, of course, it was Jesus.

We have the gospel this morning, where Mary Magdalene has gone to the disciples and apostles who have been hiding out for fear of being punished, because they were believers of Jesus. Tradition tells us that they were locked in their upper room. Mary went and told them, "Indeed he is risen. He is not in the tomb!" So, John, Peter and Mary come back to the tomb again, but they didn't find Jesus. He was gone.

In the final gospel, we find Jesus walking with two strangers who were totally consumed with the stories of the last 48 hours of the passion and death of Jesus. These guys were on their way to Emmaus and when Jesus appeared, they saw him as a stranger. He asked them what they were talking about and they said, "We are talking about all the events that have happened in Jerusalem. Are you the only one who doesn't know what happened?" It was only later, in the breaking of the bread, as scripture tells us, that they began to understand and discover that this person they had been talking with on the journey was Jesus.

I suggest that you and I find ourselves in the same predicament as all of these people and these characters in the Gospels, especially as we approach the empty tomb. We don't know where they have laid him. We don't know where Jesus is. Oh, we know the story all right. We can repeat the story almost verbatim. Yet, when it comes down to our own spiritual journey and where we find ourselves today, there is a void. When it comes down to the element of faith, our ability to believe in a mystery that we don't understand, we are challenged just like Mary Magdalene, and Mary, and Thomas and the other apostles. In fact, all of us who profess to be Christians in some fashion, sooner or later come to this moment where we have to ask ourselves "Where have *I* laid him*?*" "Where have *I* put Jesus in my spiritual lineup of priorities?"

So it is good for us to reflect on these Gospels today, at this Easter celebration. It makes the Easter experience relevant for each one of us. Maybe we need to pause and take time to think about our own lives as we exist now, where we have been and what we are dealing with, where we are finding happiness and satisfaction, and where we can find peace and understanding. Really, where do we find the things we so desperately need to feed ourselves spiritually? And then we ask ourselves the question: Is our current source of spiritual nourishment satisfying to us, or do we need to go back and find something else?

There is a paradox in Christianity. We despise or fear death, we try to alleviate pain and suffering and we try to keep ourselves in a tranquil position, spiritually, physically and mentally. Yet, the paradox is that it is only when we embrace death, we embrace pain, and we embrace our sufferings and disappointments, that we really find the answer in faith. When we embrace that which we are often told we need not experience, and we embrace it even though we do not understand it, we will find that we grow closer to the door of the Resurrection.

This is the challenge for all of us. This is the challenge that has been given to every Christian since the first Resurrection. So, we are celebrating today a feast of discovery. Of being able to discover where we are. Of being able to attempt to find what we are looking for. And ultimately, to find that when we embrace death, in its many forms, we indeed find freedom. This is what Christ has given to us. It is a free gift. All we have to do is reach out and grab it, physically and emotionally. That's what faith is all about.

As we celebrate this Easter, 2004, in a world that is so torn with all kinds of confusion, difficulties and wars, it is most appropriate for us to pause and find out where we are. Not that we blame anyone. We just start with ourselves, and try to find out where *we* have laid Jesus.

Lunge Down the Road

Philippians 3:8-14
John 8:1-11

Every week we gather and we reflect on at least two, if not three, readings from Sacred Scripture. Many times these readings are unfortunately taken out of context. Sometimes we have a hard time putting the true meaning of the passage into its proper place. Other times we find that the passage stands by itself. When I first studied scripture at college in the seminary, we had an old black bible. Everybody had the same type. When I got my bible, I thought to myself, "Well, it is all there! It's all right in this little book." I guess that was our approach in those days.

But there has been a tremendous change in the study of scripture over the past one hundred and fifty years. A lot of new insights from copies of new translations and various discoveries have taken place. With the sciences of archeology, anthropology and linguistics, together with theology, we are now getting a wonderful exegesis, or understanding, of what we know of scripture. We don't know much and/or don't speak much about the ancient discovery, the Nag Hammadi collection that was made in Egypt around 1945. There, in an old synagogue, an old room that had been plastered over contained a lot of original scrolls and second edition scrolls of the Christian message.

There were some very significant finds in the latter part of the 1800s and into the 1900s. Maybe the one that we know the most about happened between 1947 and 1956 in Qumran, a place east of Jerusalem. These Dead Sea scrolls, which were made on copper and then on vellum were hidden around the year 72, because of the destruction of the temple in Jerusalem. They had been hidden in clay jars for centuries. With the advent of all these bits and pieces, we can have a comparison between what we know today and what was given and taught centuries ago.

To really be able to appreciate scripture as scripture, we have to realize that it was first spoken, not written. It was spoken and everyone knew the stories. If there was an error in the telling of the story then it was immediately corrected by the group. The authenticity was always maintained. To the point that, when we do a serious study and comparison between our scripture of today and the translations of fragments and pieces from recent finds, we find very few, if any, discrepancies.

We have also discovered that these spoken words were to particular people at a specific time for a reason. It was the condition or the message of the time that needed to be addressed. So the teacher (Matthew, Mark, Luke or John) spoke to the individuals in the words that we know as the gospels today. They varied. There are some segments of the story, whether they be parables or events, that are found in one or the other of the gospels. Some stories are not in all of the gospels. Others are found in several of the gospels.

The reason I bring this up is that the gospel we have today is only found in the Gospel of John. And there is a reason for that. You have to remember that the first gospel that was collected and written down was Matthew's gospel. And then Mark's, Luke's and finally John's gospel, which was written around A.D. 96. Somewhere between the gospel of Luke and the gospel of John, this story of the woman taken with adultery was written. So the question comes up as to why. Why wasn't it part of the other canons of scripture? The reason is speculation, because we really don't know. But scholars do suggest that perhaps it wasn't pertinent to the time. The message of Matthew did not need this particular story, so they didn't include it. Or, perhaps it was an issue that wasn't resolved at the time and there wasn't an answer to the particular situation. Whatever it might be, we know that by the time they translated the last Gospel of John, it was included.

This tells us, then, that there is an evolution that takes place in sacred scripture. What we have today as the Canon of Sacred

Scripture, especially in the New Testament, was finally agreed upon by consensus of the leaders of the Church at that time in the fourth century. We have to also remember that the spoken word was Aramaic, from Hebrew. And then it was translated into Greek. Then St. Jerome translated it into Latin in the fourth century. He gave us what we know today as the Latin Vulgate. This is what we call the "Catholic Scripture," i.e., the number of books and letters we include in the bible we use.

Being able to know a bit of the history about the evolution of scripture, we are also able to understand that over a period of time since the fourth century, there have been other bits and pieces that have been discovered. Sometimes people ask me about the gospel of Thomas. It is a good gospel. There are interesting stories in it. There might be part of it that is fictitious and there might be part of it that is accurate. We don't know, but we know that it hasn't been included in the Canon of the New Testament.

I mention this because it is very important for us to find the richness of scripture. Scripture is not dead by any means. Scripture is very much alive. It is alive when we take the time to read scripture, pray scripture and put it into context. And it helps to know the methods and mannerisms and practices of the time when a particular section of scripture was written.

We have a story today that is interesting because the Pharisees and the scribes are trying to trap Jesus. They bring a woman who has been caught in adultery to Jesus. They are asking Jesus, "What would you do?" One of the reasons why this story has been added to the gospel of John is because it speaks of the ministry of Jesus. When you read the gospel of John, you find out that the main themes are love, forgiveness and a proper place for the law. The law is not the beginning and the end of all things! It is a system of wide parameters that allows for a gray area, as opposed to some writers of the law who say that the law is primary in the life of anyone. Jesus didn't teach that. This story backs up that opinion.

This story tells us of a woman, who according to the law of Moses, was doomed to be stoned to death. But Jesus didn't judge her like that. In fact, he simply turned the whole story around on the accusers and said, "Well, you who are without sin may cast the first stone." And then he wrote on the ground. Slowly, but surely, they left. So he then said to the woman, "Where are your accusers?" She replied, "They are gone." He then said, "I don't accuse you either. I recognize your sin, but I am simply telling you not to do it again."

The second thing we realize about Jesus in this particular story is the fact that he did not act as a judge. He didn't buy into the scenario of the scribes and the Pharisees. He accepted the facts and then, as her Savior, encouraged her to go forth and to live her life without that sin.

Some people wonder what he wrote on the ground. We have people who have spent a lot of time trying to figure that one out. When I was in the seminary they said that he probably drew a fish on the ground. And you might wonder why Jesus drew a fish. The fish is a symbol of the early Christians. It is because it is an acrostic. In other words, you take the first letter of a series of words and you put them together to spell a word. In this particular case, it spells the word *ichthus,* which is the Greek word for fish. It comes from *Jesus Christ and God Savior World, Iesous christos theos uios soter* in Greek. Pure speculation! It means nothing. It is sort of a nice thing for a preacher to throw out a little Greek now and then! It sort of impresses the folks! But it means nothing. We don't know what Jesus drew on the ground.

What we do know is the way Jesus handled the situation. Jesus handled it by saying "Stop doing what you have been doing. Be free. You are forgiven." Now, is this a new message? No, it is not. What's in the reading before this one? Paul, in his letter makes a beautiful statement. He was an educated man and he had the best of both worlds. He was not only a Greek, but he was also a Roman. He was a rabbi and he was also trained in law. He was dynamic. He had access to anyone in any area. He was also a fanatic, both *against* Christians and *for* Christians. He had a lot of baggage after his conversion. He finally realized that this baggage was useless. So he told the people he was writing the letter to, "Get rid of your baggage. Travel light on your spiritual journey. Lunge ahead! Run, run down the road! Run to the end of the Christian journey and find peace and fulfillment."

How many times do you and I carry that baggage along? We

need to free ourselves. Just like Jesus suggested to the woman in the gospel: "Be free and lunge down the road on your Christian journey!"

So I think the gospel today is very reassuring. It is backed up by a later writing which we call the Letter of Paul. The two readings support each other. The message is as contemporary today as it was the day it was first spoken. It is a message of love and forgiveness with a proper reference to law.

For the remainder of Lent (if you haven't already) lunge down the road, with God's blessing and in his company.

There's No Protocol with God

Zechariah 9:9-10
Matthew 11:25-30

As we continue our spiritual journey in life, I think it is important for us to take time to realize that each one of us is a unique individual. That there isn't a "divine cookie-cutter" that stamps out people. That each of us has our talents, our abilities, our faults and failings that make us unique in the mind of God. This we should celebrate, because it gives us the opportunity to continue to deal with life on life's terms, as it applies to each one of us. It is important for us to celebrate who we are, with all our warts and failings, and on the other hand, with the gifts that we have been given.

The second thought I want to share with you today is the fact that there is ritual, there is custom, there is protocol that all of us have to observe on certain occasions. For example, if you were to meet the Queen of England, it is not proper for you to shake her hand unless she extends her hand to you. If you go to visit the Pope, you have certain protocol to be followed as you enter into the chambers, and you do it at a certain time according to the Swiss Guards. Even in our own relationships we have certain things that we do and we don't do that are forms of social protocol.

So protocol is something that we are aware of in the general social construct of our lives. Sometimes we fail. Sometimes we make mistakes. But it is interesting, in the first reading, that the prophet tells us that there is no protocol with God. That we don't have to stand on formality. That God loves us and walks with us on our journey. This is an old theme that is repeated over and over in the

Old Testament as a description of who God is. In this particular passage, the prophet says that God is a God of love and a God of forgiveness. That's something that we really need to think about and make part of our own concept of God.

Over a period of years I have heard a lot of people describe God from a fear standpoint. It reminds me of what I would call a contemporary parable. You know the story I am going to briefly tell you. In 1939 a movie was made. The name of the movie was *The Wizard of Oz.* If you really think about *The Wizard of Oz,* you realize that it is a story about the human experience. There are four major characters. First we see Dorothy, who is in a strange land, and who wants to go back to Kansas. She meets some very interesting people on her journey. She meets a Tin Man, who has a great need to have a heart. He can't love. He can just rattle. He has been rattling his way through life. He feels empty because he doesn't have that facility to be able to give and to love.

Dorothy comes across another character, the Scarecrow. He wants a brain. He can't think. He can't discover the appreciation of creation, or of relationship. So he searches for a brain.

Dorothy also runs into a Lion. The Lion wants courage. He is tired of being a weakling. He wants to be able to face life, embrace life, and go forward. He wants to be free. So these four characters get on the road, going to find the Wizard. They hope to find, on the way back to Kansas, a heart, a brain, and courage. The interesting thing about the story is that the closer they get to where the Wizard is, the more fear begins to take over. They are not so sure that they have the ability to make the change in their life.

While the Tin Man has always dreamed about having a heart, he is not sure he can handle having a heart. That is going to be the gift from the Wizard. The same for the Scarecrow. He is not sure he would be able to handle the brain. Maybe he is better off just existing as he is. We also see the same thing with the Lion. What is he going to do with his courage? How is he going to live with something that he has never experienced?

So there comes an element of fear to all of these characters. This element of fear many times stops us on our journey. We just simply relegate ourselves to what we've always experienced when we haven't had the opportunity to find growth.

Some of the most calming and beautiful words of Scripture are found in Matthew's Gospel today. It is an invitation that Jesus gives to all of us who are burdened and find life difficult. We don't know whether we should go and receive the gift or not, or whatever we are looking for. Jesus says: *Come to me, all of you who are burdened and find life difficult, and I will refresh you. I will refresh you by giving you my yoke.*

We often have in mind that this is one collar, made of wood, that oxen would use to carry the load. But we make a mistake when we think that it is only for one. You see, it is really for two. It's Jesus' yoke. Jesus carries his weight and he extends an invitation for us to join him. And he helps us carry our weight. We face reality, from a physical as well as a spiritual standpoint, not alone. We face reality with Jesus walking with us, carrying our burden, carrying our experience. And we are refreshed.

So, today, I think it is good for us to just simply embrace who we are, where we are, what our burden is, and to realize that we don't have to be afraid to embrace the burden. We don't embrace it alone; we embrace it with a very loving God. This loving God is giving us every opportunity to pick up the load and to continue our journey in life.

Custom? Protocol? Ritual? Sometimes the only prayer that we can say is "God help me." Maybe that is the most profound prayer that we ever say. On the other hand, the other side of that prayer-coin is "Thank God." They go hand in hand. One side depends upon the other. Thank God!

The Porcupine Homily

Isaiah 66:18-21
Hebrews 12:5-7, 11-13
Luke 13:22-30

There is an old story about two porcupines. It seems that they were both traveling along and all of a sudden there came a great snow storm. These porcupines, fearing they would freeze to death, came closer and closer together. However, they soon realized that their sharp quills kept them apart. But as the snow continued, they grew even closer together. It became a very painful experience, trying to find warmth as their quills entered the skin of each other. So they parted. And there, together, they suffered through the cold and the snow.

I think it is safe to say that all of us have good points: we may be talented, gifted, energetic, committed. We have been blessed indeed. We have all of these dimensions that are part and parcel of life as we experience it today. But, like the porcupines, we have some very sharp points. These sharp points keep us apart. There are differences of opinion, of attitudes, of ways of doing things that we really don't resolve. We just simply form an opinion, based on misinformation.

Some of these sharp points are very serious. They might have to do with gender, or with religion, or with education, or money. It could even be as silly as "I don't like Brussels sprouts. You like Brussels sprouts. So, we can't be friends!" Now that is a pretty silly reason not to be able to overlook something. Yet, there is among us, as well as among all people, that sense of difference. It is a challenge that you and I have to face if we are going to go anyplace as Christian people. It calls upon each of us to enter into something that isn't too attractive. And that is a sense of discipline.

If you want to call this homily *The Porcupine Homily*, you can. But the more accurate title of the homily today is *The Discipline of Inclusion.* Mahatma Gandhi, in his autobiography, tells of his experience in reading the Gospels. He was fascinated with what he was learning. He found that he was attracted to Christianity. He wanted to find out more about it. He decided to visit a Christian Church. He was greeted by an usher who said, "You don't belong here. You are an Indian. Go over to your own church!" So, he left. And in leaving, he came to the conclusion that Christians have a caste system in their beliefs. The Indians have a caste system in their beliefs. So he concluded: "What is the difference?"

The first reading today speaks of the community of God. It speaks of all people coming together. It speaks of people who are all involved in one relationship with God. They may be people that you and I don't associate with, perhaps because we don't respect them or tolerate them. Yet, as the message of the Old Testament tells us, we are all the community of God. It also speaks of the need for us to be able to rise above the security we find in relationships and in situations that prevent us from embracing other people.

In the second reading today, we speak of the sense of discipline. Who likes to be disciplined? Who likes to enter into discipline? That is hard business. Discipline comes from a Latin word that means disciple. It means that we learn, over a period of time, to understand someone else's opinion or someone else's way of doing things. So many times we are too frightened, so we hold on tenaciously to our own opinion and we don't give the benefit of the doubt to the other. Because we don't enter into this dialogue, we learn nothing. We stay in our own limited frame of reference.

Jesus says that we have to enter into this discipline. He uses another example in the "door" image in the Gospel. If ever you have been to the Holy Land or to Europe, you will find that in the great buildings there are great, wide, wooden doors that open. Also, within one of the doors there is a small door. When there are large crowds, everyone passes through the large doors. You can carry anything with you. But if you have to go through the small door, you go through one person at a time and you can't carry anything with you. You can't bring luggage with you, because there is no room.

What Jesus is saying is that as we travel through life, we have to be able to travel light. We need to know where we are going, what we are going to be experiencing, and how we can best get to where we want to go. Jesus says that it is only then that we find a place at the table in God's kingdom. Many of us can become self-righteous and we say, "Well, after all, I've done this and that, and I've done a lot for the church, and for the government and for the community, etc." Therefore, I have the right to knock on the door, as the Gospel says this morning, and say, "Get up and let me in!" But the voice on the inside will say, "I don't know you." "Well sure you know me! You know me because we have eaten together. We have drunk together. I've listened to you teach." The voice from inside still says, "I don't know you."

Why doesn't God know us? God doesn't know us because we stay in our own stupor. Because we continue to build walls around us that prevent us from looking beyond and trying to understand another person's position, or another person's way of life. And it is not easy for us to give up that control or that perceived freedom

So, the challenge today is for us to look at the barriers, to look at those things that separate us and that we hold on to tenaciously. There are so many spin doctors in our lives today that we are literally covered up with misinformation and information about everything, whether it be church, politics, world events or what-have-you. I have to say that there is no simple answer. And there is no single issue that is paramount over another issue. The life we live today is very complicated. We need wisdom enough to realize that, as well as the time and the counsel and the opportunity to look beyond the barriers.

This is what Jesus was talking about. We have to accept this challenge. Then the doors will be opened to us. As Jesus said to the ancient Jews, "You are going to be disappointed when you don't find Abraham, Isaac, and Jacob and all the prophets coming to the banquet. You are going to find strangers in the north, south, east and west coming, because they took the opportunity to enter into the discipline of inclusion." That is our challenge also.

Hans Kung, the popular theologian of the past century, who wrote the book, *Why I am Still a Christian*, said that when all is said and done, perhaps what we really need in our world today is a good exorcism. A good exorcism means that we yell out, at the top of our voices, "Get out of here, evil spirits!" And then, let the Spirit of God come upon us. And enrich us and break down the barriers that keep us apart. Maybe, Hans Kung was absolutely right. What an event that would be.

Awareness of Our Mission

Mark 9:39-48

I suggest that human nature is the same yesterday, today and tomorrow. When you and I take the opportunity to really look at the characters of the New Testament, more particularly the apostles, we find that their human nature and their own human foibles surface. I'm not sure, if I were to receive an invitation to come over and have dinner with the twelve apostles, that I would accept that invitation. Especially if it happened before the time of the resurrection. The probability is that one would be trying to outdo the other. There would be arguments. There would be serious discussions. I personally think that I wouldn't enjoy the evening.

The reason I suggest this is because of last week's gospel as well as the one this week. If you remember, last week we read that when Jesus was coming out of a period of seclusion and prayer he was traveling up to Capernaum and he overheard the apostles and they were in a deep conversation. He said to them, "What are you talking about?" They wouldn't tell him. He said, "Well I know what you were talking about. You were discussing who would be the most important in my kingdom." Here they were, like a bunch of kids, arguing over seniority within Jesus' community!

Then we come to this particular gospel today. John comes running up and says, "Jesus, look! Someone is doing good! And he isn't part of our group. How can this be? We have the market on doing good! This person is driving out demons." They acted like a bunch of teenagers, all the way through the crucifixion, death and resurrection of Jesus. I'm not too sure they ever really learned the message of Jesus Christ, what he was about, what his mission was, until well after the resurrection. Probably on the Feast of Pentecost they began to get a glimmer of what was really going on.

Think about those people for a minute. They were fishermen. They had menial jobs. They were captivated by this very interesting man named Jesus. He had plenty of attraction; he accepted them as they were. They had risen in the eyes of their neighbors and their community. They were part of the inner circle of Jesus. They felt good, and important, for the first time in their lives. So they naturally got into such arguments as to who was the most important among them. Or they wanted to protect their territory and the mission of Jesus.

Jesus had said, "Anyone who is doing good in my name can't be stopped." So they had an awful lot to learn. You also remember that they were scared to death of the crucifixion. They ran off and hid. Remember that they were in a locked room when Jesus appeared to them the first time after his resurrection. He tried to reassure them again when he said, "Peace be to you."

Then he goes on in the gospel today and tries to use shock treatment, and tell them that they have got to understand what they are about and what his mission is. He tells them that if it is their foot that is causing them to sin, to cut it off. If it is their eye that is getting them into trouble, then they should cut it out. "All these things mean nothing compared to what I am trying to bring to you and to others." They just didn't understand what he was trying to say.

When we reflect on their personalities, where they were and what they were doing, I think many times we can see ourselves. We can find that we have acted in a similar way. It is important for us to have our name in lights, so to speak. I remember years ago, when I first started counseling and doing therapy, there was a psychiatrist who was part of our support group on Mondays. He had suffered three heart attacks. He said that he had decided that when he was out of medical school and had received his license to practice psychiatry, all he wanted was his name in lights. So he became driven to have that happen, which probably caused the heart attacks.

And here I was, a young priest sitting there, listening to

him. I thought to myself, "That's not a bad idea. I can see it now: JERRY EIFLER. If not in lights, then why not in the newspaper!" It is something that gives us, in our own estimation, stature. Did you ever notice that if something like that happens to us, then we want it to happen again and again? It eventually diverts us from what we are about. As Christian people, what are we about? Getting our name in lights? No. What we are about is our spiritual journey.

This thing that we conjure up about being important in these situations is all a figment of our imagination. It diverts us from the very basic message of Jesus Christ, just as it diverted the apostles and the disciples. It is a very simple and humbling thing for us to come together and to realize who we are by baptism and what our mission is.

Our mission is to go forth and live a life of peace and love and surrender. To simply go ahead and be aware of each other.

The message of the gospel today has to do with who we are and what we are about. I think it is good for us to ponder our own demons, those things that take us from the path—the excuses that we make for not taking the opportunity to become more involved in our own spiritual life. A lot of us are card-carrying Catholics. We'll go to our grave carrying that card that says *Roman Catholic.* I used to have a distant relative who said he was a very important Catholic, and his card said, "In case of death, call the Bishop."

The message of today is strong. It asks us to consider our motives. It asks us to think about who we are and what we are about, and to realize that what we have is the love, protection and salvation that were given to us through baptism by Jesus Christ.

Travel Light

Luke 10:1-12, 17-20

Just as last Sunday, we have again this week the "Travelogue according to Luke." You may recall that last week, the Gospel centered around three points. First, that life is a journey. We have the past, the present and the future. Not only are we talking about a physical journey, but also about a spiritual journey. The second point of last week's lesson was that this journey is not an easy one. There are various obstacles and challenges as we go along. We do not travel alone; we travel with Christ and with each other. As we travel, we reach out and we support each other. The third point had to do with the stuff that we bring along with us. The stuff is usually stuff that we have inherited. It may be addiction, dysfunction, low self-esteem and/or various other aspects that we have to deal with sooner or later. We are challenged to let it go and to travel light.

Today, our Gospel talks about the attitude of travel. I would suggest that the first part of the reading is more figurative than it is practical. The story in Luke tells us that Jesus has gathered 72 disciples and sent them out in pairs to go on their journey. He instructs them not to take anything along with them. "Don't take your moneybag. Don't take an extra pair of sandals. Don't take an extra cloak, etc." What he is really implying is that as we go into the unknown, it is important to be open to the experience. We don't need to take everything we have with us, because it might block what we are going to discover on the journey.

It is similar for a first trip one might take abroad. We read the magazines and travel books and try to learn as much as we can about the customs, the money and all the rest. But the first time we go abroad can be an awkward experience because we don't know what to expect. We are going into the unexpected when we leave our familiar habitat and go forward. So Jesus suggests that as the disciples go forward, they go with an open mind. They need to trust each other that things will work out.

Once we go on our journey and we are out of our own environs, we find ourselves at the mercy of others. We find that we have to be open to the hospitality of others. Even though we would rather do it ourselves, we have to be dependent on others for our food, word translation, directions, etc. Who among us likes to be dependent? We like to be independent and have things well ordered, don't we? But that's not the way the journey is.

Then, as we go into the villages, we are going to receive kindness. People are going to give us directions, point us to the right train, etc. And we are going to have to reciprocate in kind. We are going to have to be able to receive graciously, and also extend a hand of welcome to others as we continue this journey. The spiritual life has to do with the same kind of things: being dependent upon one another, being hospitable, receiving other people's generosity and being able to return favors to others as we go along. Yet, when you and I are on our own, we feel more comfortable. But I'm not too sure that we get the benefit of the travel.

I think a modern parable might be appropriate at this time. The first time I went to Europe and to Rome, I think I came face to face with an individual who is known as the "Ugly American." I describe the ugly American as someone who is fearful, who hasn't prepared well for travel to a foreign land and who doesn't know what is appropriate. They come in like gangbusters and they expect everyone to act the way they act at home. And it is just not that way.

The first day we were in Rome, we took a tour of the "Old Town" of Rome. In the afternoon, we took a tour of the more modern Rome. We were told to be very prompt for the tours. We were picked up for the first tour and went to the next stop. We waited and waited and finally the last passenger descended upon our group. She was covered with an immense flowered dress and she had a beehive hairdo. She had cat-eye glasses with rhinestones on them. She had two cameras hanging around her neck and a pad and pencil under her arm. She was ready to attack Rome. She was late, but that didn't bother her.

We continued on the bus route, and the tour guide gave an explanation of where we were going and what we were going to see. She was paying no more attention to the guide than anything else that was going on in life. We went to a great church called St. Mary Major. She was near me and she asked me what the name of the church was. I repeated what the guide had told us and she answered, "Oh, St. Mary Magdalene Church" and wrote that down! She took tons of pictures of this church that she had misidentified. We were sort of relieved when she left the tour.

Lo and behold, who showed up at the afternoon tour with her cameras and pad but our American friend! We went to many places and finally to the Catacomb of Priscilla. It is a very old catacomb on the Appian Way. We were greeted by a distinguished Englishman who was going to be our escort. We were down deep in the catacombs and the guide came across this slab that had *Alexandrius* on it. He told us that it was an unopened tomb of Alexander, a man buried around the third century. She came along afterwards and said, "Sir, is this the tomb of Alexander the Great?" He replied, "Madam, anyone buried here had to be great."

Now I felt sorry for that woman, because she really didn't prepare for the trip. I could only imagine what would happen when she came home and showed all of her pictures to her friends and tried to explain what she had seen. She missed the whole experience. And you and I can miss the whole experience of life when we have only our own agendas, when we don't take the time to savor the uniqueness of the position or the place that we happen to be in. That lady's tour could have been life-giving, if only she would have been open to the possibility of just a few pictures, of listening closely to the guide, of being able to savor this unique experience. But that wasn't her take.

Unfortunately, the same thing happens to us. That's what Jesus was saying to people in the Gospel today. He said, "When you go off, don't be distracted by a lot of stuff. When you come across someone who is hospitable, accept their hospitality. When you leave, extend a blessing to them and go on your journey. That's the way you and I are to travel through life, not only physically, but spiritually.

This frantic pace that we keep many times clouds anything we find that might nourish us. Somewhere, somehow, we have to put the brakes on. We have to learn how to savor the moment.

There is another important point that we need to consider. We have to recognize that our world is getting smaller. It is important for us to get to know each other, to appreciate the heritage and the uniqueness of each other, and to support each other in love and respect. So many times, when we travel, we find there are people who have to be "The Great American." They project the attitude that we are much better than anyone else in the world.

But we are human beings. And we need love just like anyone else needs love. We need respect just like anyone else needs respect. If we are so great, then we have to extend that greatness to others. We have to make sure that we convey our appreciation of their presence and their history.

There is a perceived attitude about Americans abroad. Many times we create that attitude when we get in conversations about how great and how large our country is. We aren't great because we are mighty. We are great because we have the ability to appreciate others, because we can extend love and peace to others and because we can recognize their history, which is many thousands of years older than ours.

So my friends, on our journey, whether it is in our physical life or in our spiritual life, we have a lot to learn. Just because we are proud of who we are or where we live, doesn't mean that we can convey to others that they are less than we are.

Today, as we celebrate Independence Day and the gifts that were given to us as a nation by those who gained independence for us, it is important for us to recall not only the physical journey analogy, but more important, the spiritual journey analogy of realizing that all of us are the same. We have the same needs, whether we are in Bangladesh, or Italy, or South America, or in Louisville, Kentucky. We have the same ability to love and the same need to be loved.

So I hope you have a good day of remembrance, a good day of evaluation, a good day of independence. May your prayer be to see that others gain the same freedom and the same independence that we have.

Why *Not* Bethlehem?

Micah 5:1-4a

We know very little about the preparation for Jesus' coming from the Old Testament. We have the words of the prophet Micah in today's first reading. He identifies the place of birth as Bethlehem. But he hastens to say that Bethlehem is not one of the shining stars in the constellation of the kingdom of Israel. We also have that line from scripture that reads: "God will send the Savior in the fullness of time." What does that mean, "the fullness of time?" Basically it means in God's good time. It was when God deemed it necessary for Christ to be born.

But the question that has always been in my mind is "Why Bethlehem?" Bethlehem wasn't much. It was only 5 miles from Jerusalem. It was just sheep pens and pasture, which was very poor land. It was populated by some shepherds. They had an industry there. They raised sheep so that the people who were making their way to Jerusalem to offer sacrifices could buy their sheep there, take it to the sheep pool where it was cleansed, and then go to the Temple. That was the sole purpose of Bethlehem. It had very little, if any, other industry. Even today, if you have ever been to Bethlehem, it is not much of a town. If it weren't for the church that they attribute to the Nativity, which was reconstructed by the Crusaders, no one would be there.

Now, there is Manger Square, which is open according to the political situation, where they will sell you stoles woven by the Bedouins, or statues and trinkets carved out of olive wood. But that's about it. When you really think about it, why *was* Jesus born in such an insignificant place? Just think of the options. Rome, for example—all roads came to Rome, the international city of the time, where people from every corner of the world were meeting. There was a great sense of the financial, political, and intellectual dealings that took place there.

If not Rome, then why wasn't it Athens, the home of Aristotle, Plato and Socrates? Athens was the seat of the world of philosophy at the time. It could even have been Alexandria in Egypt. What a place! At the time of Christ they had a library there that contained six hundred thousand manuscripts that were lent to the people. Three hundred years before the time of Christ, in Alexandria, they had the Poet's Corner. They had places where the poets would come and lecture to the people, so it was the hub of the intellectual activity of the world. There were great cities that surrounded this menial little place called Bethlehem.

So why Bethlehem? I've thought about this a lot over the years. Even today, without the tradition of the Nativity, it would still be that miserable little town it was when Jesus was born.

You know, there is no way that you and I can live up to the expectations of Christmas. It is bigger than all of us put together. You go to the mall. You go to the center of big cities like Chicago and you walk down Michigan Avenue and you see all the lights at Tiffany's, Neiman Marcus, Bloomingdale's and all the people gathered around their windows. There is no way that you and I can live up to that expectation.

When I was a little kid, I found myself sort of depressed on Christmas evening. It was only much later when I reflected upon it that I realized that I had this image of what a Christmas should be. And my Christmases at home were wonderful. We weren't deprived of anything. We had excess. But yet, it was never enough in the imagination. When you really get down to it, preparing for Christmas as we do today amounts to a lot of menial tasks. You have to select a card. Then you get the card list out. Then you have to correct the card list. People have died, they have divorced, they have gotten married, they have moved. So you have to edit the whole thing. And I don't know anybody who gets any pleasure of doing that. But you've got that issue to take care of.

Then, if you are going to have the family, you have to prepare the meal. You have to get out the old recipes, you have to look for this one or that one. (I'm still looking for one that I need for Thursday myself.) Then you put up some decorations. You put out the same old decorations you've had for years. One more time you'll put them up, but you'll add a few fresh ones this time. Then you plug the lights in and they don't work. So then you do the menial job of taking the lights out and testing them to see which one doesn't work. And the tasks go on and on.

That's what we are about. Somehow, it all fits. The menial tasks fit into the celebration of Christmas. And I suggest that they fit because that's what you and I do in the course of living out our lives. We go to the same mailbox to get our mail, day in and day out. We get the groceries at the same place. We drive the same routes to work and back. We greet the same people we are working with. We know the tasks that are expected of us in the marketplace or at home. After a while, it all sort of gets ordinary, doesn't it? Life gets ordinary. And then we live for that day when we can retire. We can go into this fantasy land where we can see ourselves off someplace doing other things, and there will be no menial tasks.

I suggest this morning that maybe the reason why God picked the ordinary place of Bethlehem was because that was a symbol of the mission of Jesus. After all, he didn't select the powerful of the community to be in his group. He picked the ordinary fishermen, who were just as bored with their jobs as we may be with ours. He didn't go ahead and heal the wealthy, or the prominent, or the intellectuals. He spoke to the ordinary folks.

When we reflect on that aspect of Jesus' mission, he brought the saving grace that Micah speaks of in the first reading today. Micah tells us that it was going to happen at Bethlehem and that the payoff was going to be peace. So I think it means that we have to be faithful to the ordinary things that we do in the course of living out our lives. We have to be faithful to putting up the tree, faithful to celebrating the feast, faithful to extending the gifts, faithful to receiving the gifts, faithful to letting ourselves listen to the Christmas carols. But it is all on our terms.

We can never live up to the expectations of what Madison

Avenue tries to tell us: that we will receive the ultimate, and that when we receive the ultimate, we will be happy. That is a false message. The ultimate will never make us happy. It can't make us happy. I often ask myself, "When is enough enough?" I've never met a person who can answer that question. That's not where we find happiness. That's not where we find peace. That's not where we find love. We find it in the ordinary tasks of living. That's where Jesus brought his message. Then it seems logical that he wouldn't be caught dead in Rome. He wouldn't be caught dead in Athens. He had no reason to go to Alexandria. All he needed was a group of people who were in need. And what he had to give was his love. At the end of the day, that is what makes us happy.

Close Encounter with Faith

John 20:19-31

As we gather these next few weeks to celebrate the season of Easter, I think it is important for us to realize that the season of Easter has to do with *encounter*. We see in the reading of the Gospel that through fear the disciples hid out, not knowing what was in their future— whether they were to be arrested also, and tortured and put to death because they were followers of Jesus. But when Jesus appeared in their midst, he said, "Peace be to you." He gave them a sense of well-being. He gave them a sense of security. He gave them peace.

The disciples accepted it on faith. They didn't know what in the world had happened. The last they knew was that their Master was crucified and buried. And they were on the run. But then he appears and says "Peace." They take that greeting of peace on faith, and this turns their life around. Over a period of time they start their journey, and they find themselves giving testimony to the dimension of life that you and I have as Christian people: regardless of how we find ourselves or where we find ourselves or what we are dealing with, there is in God's world a sense of peace, a sense of blessing, a grace to face the reality of where we are.

Over a period of years, there have been many preachers who have taken each line of the story of Easter and the Resurrection and tried to analyze it, making a great point of John running before Peter to get to the tomb, about the angels saying that Christ is not there, about Mary Magdalene meeting the gardener and not recognizing him as Jesus, and so on. In my estimation they have missed the whole meaning of what Easter is all about.

Easter isn't about the *incidents* of the story. What Easter is about is what Jesus brings to his people. And that is well-being and a sense of peace. How many of us do not have our own fears? We all have fears. There is not one human being who has ever drawn a breath who has not had fears to deal with: fear of being rejected, fear of being abandoned, of being misunderstood, of trying to start something and make it a success, fear of failure, fear of being left without enough to survive. All these fears, when we allow them to grow in our own minds, can ultimately paralyze our journey. Because we are so fearful of what might happen, the risk of entering into the posture of faith is just not possible.

So many times we go through life and try to resurrect a sense of well-being. We try to believe in what Jesus says to us, but we just don't get it. Faith hasn't developed enough within our own being that we can actually say, "Yes, I believe that God will take care of me in spite of all of the things that I have surrounded my life with to protect me from harm." When we can let go of the fears that really govern our lives, then we are able to stand tall and realize what faith is all about.

Faith is believing in the well-being that God gives us through the Resurrection. You and I enter into a number of deaths each day. We die over and over again, whether it is in a misunderstanding, the loss of a friendship, or something minor or major. Whatever it is, we experience these little deaths. They chip away at our well-being, but we withstand them, one way or another. All of these little deaths lead us to *the* death, the passing from this life to the next.

What Jesus is really saying in the Resurrection is that we have the opportunity to encounter the element of faith, in his presence and through the many people we come in contact with. We find testimony through the mystery of Easter.

So that's what it is about. It's not about eggs and whether John beat Peter to the tomb. It is not even about the story of Thomas in the Gospel today. That is a good example of a transition from fear to faith. And then Thomas living out his life in testimony to that belief is wonderful, but that event is not the essence of Easter.

I spent yesterday in Bowling Green, Kentucky. I was invited to be part of a Kentucky Author's Workshop that is held annually. I had never been to one before, but I took some of my books and went and was given a station in a row of many authors. There were probably 150 to 200 authors there from around the state and surrounding states. It was a very interesting experience. I guess I didn't realize that there are so many books published about so many different subjects just in this area.

The most interesting title I found from a quick perusal of the offerings was a book entitled "Who Cooked the Last Supper?" I immediately thought of Tommie O'Callaghan and knew that she would appreciate it, so I have a copy for you, Tommie! I'm not going to talk about how many books I sold. I'll just tell you that I have some left.

Next to me was a man known as the "Laugh Doctor." He is Cliff Kuhn, a very talented man. You may know him. He attracted a lot of attention by wearing a red rubber nose. I didn't have any props. I was just there, with my book. A couple next to me was offering a book entitled "The Holiness Churches of Appalachia." It is a fascinating book! They have researched all of the little, single room churches in Appalachia, and over in Virginia and West Virginia, about their Christian beliefs and their manner of worship, snake handling, and other such things.

Pat, the wife of the author, was telling me about this group of people whom they went to visit, who had the practice of "singing down" the preacher. The preacher would start. He would preach on and on and on. And when the people had enough they would start singing and they would sing until they had out-sung him. Finally he would sit down. I thought that this was really a novel idea and I wondered if I could apply this idea to St. Frances of Rome!

But that wasn't the point. Pat and her husband Warren had a story. Pat was in a rather large electric wheelchair. She rode over and picked up my book. She parked right in front of my space, making it difficult for anyone else to pick up a book. She said, "Oh, I see you are a priest." I said, "Yes." Then she said, "I am an ordained minister also. I was campus minister for Berea College for quite a few years." She went on to tell me that she majored in theology at Transylvania in Lexington. She said she also did counseling at Berea College. She was very lovely. She went on to speak of her own faith journey.

Pat and Warren went off for a while and eventually he came back to their station. Then Warren came over to me and said, "Pat really enjoyed talking to you. I would like to buy your book and I ask you to write an inscription in it to her. And by the way, put a prayer in there too." So I wrote something for her. Then I said to him, "Tell me about Pat. How long has she been disabled?"

Warren answered, "She has been this way for about fifteen years. She had a violent viral infection that got into her spinal column, and she was paralyzed from the waist down overnight." He went on to say that he takes her with him everywhere he goes. He said, "She is very active. She still conducts funerals and weddings."

I said that I was just amazed at her attitude about things. He said, "It is really a blessing, isn't it? She's taking a nap now. We have rearranged our lives around her disability, but our lives are still very full." I sat there, and I thought about Pat. I thought about the homily I was going to give this weekend and I thought, "What a gift!" This person, who is now a friend, who is faced with such a debilitating experience, who lives in this wheelchair day in and day out, who is blessed with a loving husband who is able to take care of her needs, and three children who come and help with her exercises, is not daunted in her ministry or in her faith and she is able to give testimony.

That's what it is all about! That's what the Easter mystery is about! It's about those opportunities that you and I have, like in coming across someone in a wheelchair in Bowling Green, Kentucky who is alive and who radiates love and kindness. She had a wonderful smile on her face. She didn't need a red rubber nose! She was just present. Present to me and to everyone who passed by. She apparently believes that there is nothing to fear, and she demonstrates that in so many ways.

That is the latest example I've had that has renewed and redirected my thinking about where my fears are and how I deal with them; about how my faith is and how I deal with that; about my attempt to rise above my fear, to be able to testify to the reality of what Jesus told the early Christians initially when they saw him, "Fear not. Peace be with you."

I came home after carrying my books down there and back, and selling only a few. But let me tell you, I came home a wealthier man for having gone to Bowling Green, and being in the path of Pat and Warren, than if I had sold all of my books.

That is the Easter encounter. Look for it. Celebrate it. And continue the journey.

Be Open

Matthew 4:12-23

We are celebrating what is known as the Third Sunday in Ordinary Time, which is really a section between the Christmas Season and Lent. So we call this Ordinary Time. In this cycle of Sacred Scripture we are following the Gospel of Matthew. We are in the third chapter. If you remember, the last couple of Sundays we have been talking about John the Baptist, the concept of Baptism, and Jesus' Baptism. Now, we find that Jesus, having left his hometown of Nazareth, has moved to Capernaum.

It is good for us to remember that there were many people baptizing at the time of Jesus' ministry. It was an ordinary thing. People would come to be bathed, to be cleansed, so that they would not catch a disease. Disease had to do with sin. So if there was a washing or a baptism, then it was a cleansing of the body and they were then free from disease, and therefore free from sin. People believed that sin was a punishment from God, in the form of sores and disfigurement such as leprosy. John was baptizing and many people came, not from a spiritual standpoint as much as a practical standpoint. He saw Jesus. He knew about Jesus. John said to him, "I am not worthy to baptize you." But Jesus said, "No, you have to cleanse me." And in this cleansing, different from all the rest, a voice was heard: "This is my Beloved Son upon whom my favor rests."

So we see that it is a different kind of washing or cleansing. With this, Jesus began his public ministry. Now he wasn't accepted in Nazareth, where he had grown up. Twice he got into difficulty with the authorities. They were amazed the first time when he got up and spoke with elegance after he had proclaimed the Scripture. They were saying to each other, "Where did he get all of this? Isn't he simply the son of Joseph, a carpenter in our community?"

The second time Jesus challenged them as neighbors and family, they said, "He is just too much for us." Scripture says they took him to the brow of the hill and they were going to stone him. Instead, he walked through their midst and left. So, the natural question is, "Where did Jesus go?"

He moved. He left the town of Nazareth and went up to a fabulous place called Capernaum. That is where we find Jesus in the Gospel today. We have read the third chapter of Matthew, where Jesus starts calling forth his disciples. If you were to go to Capernaum today, you would be amazed at the beauty of the place. There are lush fields, great almond groves and wonderful fruit orchards. It is an idyllic place.

What you see there now are remnants and reminders of the places where Jesus met his people. The house of Peter, for example, is right across the road from the synagogue where he preached. All you have are black basalt foundation stones, but they are there. There is a lot of tradition that speaks of Jesus and his ministry in this town.

So Jesus goes out for a walk and he sees some fishermen. He sees all of the activity of the community and he comes upon these two individuals, Peter and Andrew. He approaches them and says, "Come follow me. Become my disciples." They immediately leave their nets and follow him. He goes on a little further and he sees two other brothers, James and John, Zebedee's sons. They were mending their nets in the boat. He said, "Come follow me." They, too, left their father and came over to him. Obviously, Jesus was a very charismatic individual. He drew people to him.

He looks at the four men who have come over to him and says: "Repent, for the kingdom of God is at hand." You and I, when we hear the word repent, think about the Sacrament of Reconciliation perhaps. Or abstaining from food for forty days. But that is not what Jesus meant at all. What he asked of these four men is the same thing that he asks of you and me today. He asks that we open our minds and our hearts and our spirits to the voice of God. He calls the men disciples. The word disciple comes from the Latin word, *discipulus,* which means a student; one who is in the process of learning.

What Jesus is really calling us to do on our spiritual journey is to take all the stuff that we know—our prejudices, our opinions, the things that we are *so* convinced of—set them aside and become teachable. Become teachable in the form of the Spirit that is within us through baptism. This act of baptism was not simply a washing that you and I went through. It was a gift of the Spirit. For you and I are in contact with the Spirit, who guides us. Many times our opinions and our prejudices and other issues keep us from even hearing the Word of God. We are the less for it. Because, as disciples, when we listen to the Word of God and we open our minds to it, then we begin to hear something that perhaps we hadn't heard before. We begin to evaluate and we begin to assess our life in a different way. So the invitation has been extended to these four men as they walked along the shore at Capernaum. It has come to us also.

About eight or ten years ago there were four letters that were all over the place, on bumper stickers, on billboards, in the paper, and on bracelets. These four letters were WWJD. As you know, it means *What Would Jesus Do?* This got started up in Holland, Michigan with a youth group at the Calvary Reform Church. I thought, when I heard it, that it was nice for teenagers or kids in grade school. How many times did we think it was good for us: sophisticated, middle-aged adults?

But these words could remind us to ask ourselves how we should respond to everyday, problematic situations. How do we react to the driver who cuts in front of us? What about the cashier who gives us too much change? We run into many ordinary dilemmas that we don't think of as moral problems.

When you think about applying this type of thing to ordinary living, to our human existence, which is where our spiritual life really is, then this trite little saying of WWJD begins to look different. It *is* different. It is not trite. When you really come down to it, it is pretty deep theology.

If you and I are going to be disciples, we have to set aside the stuff that we hold so dear and that we have insulated ourselves with. We have to risk being open, just like those four guys risked leaving their fathers' businesses and walked along the shore with

Jesus, not knowing where in the world they were going or what they were doing. He didn't give them a job description. He didn't give them a syllabus of all the things he was going to teach them. He just said to them, "Be Open!"

So, today, as we continue our journey, think about WWJD. Be open. Continue your journey, and I guarantee that it will make a difference in your life.

Epiphany—The Story of a Journey

Isaiah 60:1-6
Matthew 2:1-12

The story of Jesus, his birth, and the whole Christmas and Epiphany episodes are full of symbols and signs. Symbols and signs are part of life. You and I desperately need symbols and signs to get through each day. I guess it has always been that way. The symbol of the star that attracted the Magi. The Magi themselves as a symbol. The shepherds as a symbol. Bethlehem as a symbol. Mary and Joseph as a symbol. The child as a symbol. All of the elements of the nativity story are caught up in the symbol and the sign that conveys to us the insights and opportunities to discover something more about our journey.

The interesting thing that I find on the feast of the Epiphany is that it is really not a message or a sign about Magi or stars or the discovery of the Christ child. I would suggest to you this morning that it is really the story of a journey, and that all of us are on this journey. If we put ourselves back in the context of the Gospel today and the people of the Nativity scene, we'll see that everyone was coming from different places with different agendas and ideas. They all converged at this one point where Christ was manifested to his people and now to the world. That's what Epiphany means. It means Christ's manifestation to *all* people, not just the House of David, not just the house of his heritage and his lineage.

This is a challenge for us to consider, because so many times you and I live in our own little camps. We live with our friends whom we know and love and trust. We live within our community and our own nation, where we often stay throughout our lives.

I remember the first time I took a trip abroad. I was actually afraid to go because I didn't know what I was going to discover. I took twice as much stuff as I needed to take, because I had heard horror stories of not being able to buy the ordinary medicine or the ordinary necessities that you and I enjoy today. Once I got over there and went into their stores, I found that they had more stuff than we do. But that was my perception, even though, over a period of time, I have tried to be a person who does not take other people's inventory. What I mean is not to sit back and quietly make a judgment on what you perceive other people to be.

I'll give you an example: about twenty years ago I was on a subway in New York and I was going downtown. A young man got on the subway with me. He was maybe in his twenties, and pretty disheveled. He had a tee shirt on with a lot of holes in it. He had sandals and blue jeans that were worn out and dirty. And he sat adjacent to me. So there I was, sitting in my seat and wondering what rock he had crawled out from under. I was saying to myself, "Looks pretty ragged. I bet he hasn't been to bed forever." I had started the process of making the judgment, using my own interpretation as to where this individual might have been, what he was about, and did he have a gun! You can spin a wonderful web around an individual when you take their inventory.

At the next stop, after I had pretty well said in my mind that this was an unsavory individual, to say the least, another individual got on just like him. They were friends. He came over and sat with the man. I thought to myself, "Gosh, there are two of them!" I didn't really mean to overhear their conversation, but it was unavoidable. One guy said to the other, "How are you doing?" "Not well" was the answer. He said, "Why not?" "I've got a jonesin'." I didn't know what this meant at the time. I discovered later on that it is a compulsive need for a drug. I didn't know what it was, but I could tell from the conversation that it wasn't good. The guy who had just gotten on the train was sympathetic, but he said, "What are you doing about it?" The answer was, "Well, I'm not doing what I should."

The other guy then said, "Are you praying?" "Well!" I thought to myself, "praying! I'm the guy who prays! What are these bums doing?" But the guy went on to say, "Man, there is no other way you can do it. The only way you can do something about the jonesin' is by praying. Did you do your meditation this morning?"

I thought to myself, "I can't believe these guys meditate!" I had them totally wrong! The picture I had painted about these two individuals was absolutely, totally false. But I had taken their inventory. On my own, I had decided who they were, what they were about, what their contribution to society and their worth as individuals were, and all the rest. And I was wrong. I was caught up in my own role of being the pray-er, of being the one with the answers, of being the one set aside by God to do good things.

What I heard in the conversation between the young man who came on at the second stop, and the one who was in pain, was one of the most beautiful, sincere and honest concerns for another individual that I have ever heard. It was all centered around God's role and the need to be able to communicate with God through prayer and meditation. The costumes meant nothing. The pain was real for the one individual. And the person who got on the subway, and encouraged him to pray, was the one who was acting as the Christ that day.

You see, my friends, the story of Epiphany is the story of relationships. It's the relationships that you and I have with each other. But to be able to appreciate this relationship, you and I have to do something. What I think we have to do is to look at the bigger picture, to rise above the ordinary milieu that we are experiencing. We need to look at the picture that God sees.

This sort of came to me on New Year's Eve when I was sitting in my study and I was watching, from various places, New York and Times Square and other areas that were celebrating. What did I see but millions of people gathered, in a sense of safety, in a sense of jubilation, gathered there for one reason. They were there to kiss the old year goodbye and to bring in the new year. From my vantage point, way above all of them, I could see way out the boulevards of New York. I could see it all from overhead, so to speak. And that picture is entirely different from the one we get when we stand on the street with a very limited focus and we look from one place to another. We only see other individuals.

It is God's view that we have to develop. You know, all of us are going to knock on the same door sometime. God's door. The person that we minimize and criticize and overlook is going to be there too. Those people in other nations that we really don't respect, or we are frightened of, or that we don't know, are going to be there also. That's the world that we live in.

But we limit our vision. When we limit our vision, we see only the small things. And when we see the small things, nine times out of ten our interpretation is incorrect. We are great at taking each others' inventory. Wouldn't it be wonderful if, this year, we just set that awesome responsibility aside, and let people be people? And learn to look at that person in a bigger way?

The only way we can get beyond this inventory and this criticism is by looking at things the way God does. And what God sees, God loves. God calls everyone to be instruments of his peace, his love and his forgiveness. This is the Epiphany — when Christ manifests himself *to* all of us *through* all of us.

Saints of Then and Now

We are becoming more and more aware of the fact that there are certain elements of life and celebration that are important to us, whether in retrospect or in actually celebrating the events. And so it is with joy that the community gathers today to celebrate with three people who made their First Communion yesterday: Claire, Cate and Thomas.

When we think about these three people making their First Communion, it is easy for us to reflect back on when we made our First Communion. We remember how important it was to get things right. Those of you who are near my age remember how we had to make sure that we didn't break our fast, like drinking water after midnight. We had to fold our hands a certain way, like right over the left, not left over the right. There was a lot of ritual that we were made aware of. We can laugh about it now, but it was an important event. It was important then and is still important now. And this is an important event for these three young people today.

It is important for us to celebrate First Communion as a family ritual. We have our ways of celebrating birthdays, Christmas, Thanksgiving and all the rest. Sometimes, sacramental receptions have fallen by the wayside. As some say, it's "just another day." That is certainly unfair for those who need the element of ritual and passage in their lives.

We can go back to primitive tribes, and we can see that there were people set aside as mentors for the men and women, the young girls and boys, to go through their rites and passages. So it is with the tradition in our Church. We have ancient rites of passage. I was thinking about Claire, and about her namesake. Clare was a very powerful young lady. She was a contemporary of a man named Francis who lived at Assisi in Italy. He was a wealthy young man whose father was a cloth merchant. Clare and Francis were good friends. They were what you would call boyfriend and girlfriend.

Francis had an issue with the luxury of his father. He needed to break away and establish himself. He needed to be able to make a statement about something he really believed in. He discussed it with Clare. In his writings, there is a beautiful dialogue between Clare and Francis, about what he wanted to do and about how he could break out of the mold that his father had put him in so he could become the next cloth merchant in Assisi. So, he broke away, by throwing all of his father's cloths and fragments out the window of the store into the public square. He then went naked before his father and said, "I don't want anything that you have to give me."

Francis then went off and became a hermit. His friend, Clare, followed his lead. She gave away her inheritance and started a counterpart to the Franciscans. They are known as the Poor Clares. They are a religious order who stress simplicity in their daily living. They are the largest contemplative order in the world. This means that they spend time throughout the day before the Blessed Sacrament praying that we will all grow in love for God and for each other. So when our Claire comes and makes her First Communion, she brings with her the legacy of St. Clare. This is part of who she is as she receives Communion.

Then there is Cate. Cate was another faith-filled woman. She was from Siena. At that time (in the 1400s) the Pope was in France. He had lived there for some seventy-odd years, under the French king. Rome had fallen into ruin. Nothing was there. The vandals and the people from the East had sacked all of Rome. The Pope ran off and hid under the skirts of the French king.

So the papacy was in France and there was a dramatic young lady who thought that this was wrong. She thought it was time for the pope to come back to his rightful place in Rome. Her name was Catherine. She decided she was going to do something about it. She was a very prayerful person, a person given to determination.

She went to Avignon, where the pope was ensconced in the French King's palace. She talked to him and told him he needed to get away from there. She said, "You've got to get away and go back to Rome where you really belong." She decided to persuade. And so, in the story of Catherine, there is a scene where the French army was battering down the doors of the Castle of Avignon. They were beating against these great doors, and finally they made it into the chapel and there, you saw the French army coming to capture Catherine and the pope. Cate got up, walked up into the sanctuary, picked up a flaming brazier and threw it, with the coals, down the aisle at the army. It stopped them and Cate and the pope escaped.

It was because of the determination of Catherine of Siena that the pope returned to Rome. He started the whole reconstruction of Rome and started building St. Peter's and the Vatican and all the rest. Catherine died in her mid-20s. She wasn't an elderly woman when she persuaded the pope to move. So this is the legacy you bring with you today, Cate, as you receive your First Communion.

And then there was Thomas. We don't know too much about Thomas but there are a lot of legends about him. One thing we know about Thomas is that he was always asking questions. And that's just about the way our Thomas is today! He is inquisitive. He is always asking questions!

Thomas was part of the famous Twelve. He was part of the inner circle with Jesus. He was one of the Apostles. He was there, but he wanted to know more. We call him "doubting Thomas." I think this is a mistake. I think he was really the most intellectual of the whole bunch, to tell you the truth. I think he wanted to know everything there was to know about the plan of Jesus, about how things really were, and who God was, and where Jesus was going to take them.

It was Thomas who asked the right questions at the right time. And Jesus recognized that and gave Thomas a great insight into His whole mission as the Savior of the world. So Thomas wasn't just a fisherman; he was an intellectual. He was one who wasn't afraid to ask the question!

From these three people — from Claire, from Cate, and from Thomas — you and I can all ponder the gifts that have been brought to us through our tradition.

The gift of Clare calls us to evaluate what is important in

our lives. When we do this we find that it is love and peace and not material success and wealth. We learn from her actions that loving God and others is what brings real happiness.

We look at Catherine, who had such determination and conviction about her faith and about what is right and just in this world, that she overcame an army and she took a very weak pope back to Rome and saw that he was reestablished on the throne of Peter.

Then we find Thomas. Thomas, the man who asked the questions. He wasn't afraid that they might be foolish. They were questions that he needed to have answers for. And rightly so. We all have such opportunities.

And us? Do we have inquisitive minds? Do we have an inquisitive mind especially about spiritual matters, or about matters of faith, or matters of the Church as it exists today? I hope so.

So the challenge is there. People whose names we carry in the Christian calendar are all strong people. I just described three today, the patron saints of the people who just made their First Communion. God will bring to them, or to you and me, the stamina of a Clare, the dedication of a Cate, and the inquisitiveness of a Thomas. Because of these people and the people like them, we will be able to find other facets and other meanings of peace and justice, and the healing that we need in our communities today.

Now, kids, thanks for making your First Communions. We are delighted to be at your celebration.

Be Careful What You Ask For

Mark 10:46-52

Several weeks ago in our Sunday readings we had the story of Solomon and God. God said to him: "Whatever you ask for, Solomon, will be given to you. What do you want?" And Solomon said, "Of all the things that you could give me, I want the gift of wisdom." So God gave Solomon the gift of wisdom. This gift of wisdom is profound, because it is really a gift of sight and insight. It is the ability to look into a situation, an experience, or a problem and to be able to go through it piece by piece, element by element. It is the gift of being able to put into proper focus that which you are trying to see. This is the gift that God gave to Solomon. Solomon used this gift very well.

In our gospel today, we have the story of a blind man, Bartimaeus. A blind man really had no purpose or dignity at that time. He eked out an existence by begging. He was totally dependent on others for his welfare. The great prayer that Bartimaeus had was that, someday, somehow, somewhere, he might see. He knew Jesus, and he knew Jesus was a descendant of Solomon, and from the house of David. He also had heard about what Jesus had done for many others. When he found out that it was Jesus who was passing by, he was very excited. He thought, "Maybe this is my hope. Maybe my prayer can be answered."

He called out to Jesus, and Jesus responded and asked him the most significant questions of his life. "What do you want, Bartimaeus? How can I help you? What is your need? What is your dream?" Bartimaeus simply said, "I want to see." And Jesus answered,

121

"Your faith has set you free." With that, Bartimaeus was able to see.

We have often heard it said that we better make sure that we want what we pray for, because, like Bartimaeus, when we accept the gifts of sight and insight, it is going to cost us. There is no way you can get around it. The gift that you receive because you have opened your relationship with God will ultimately touch your time, your talent and your treasure. That's where we are, isn't it? We have to be prepared to make some significant changes in our lives when we go to God and ask for a gift.

The gift that we will receive will be the same gift that Bartimaeus received, from a spiritual, emotional and psychological point of view. Maybe even from a physical point of view. This gift will change our lives. It will challenge us to realize that most of the time we have spent our life at the altar of ego and speed. The most significant and the most profound gift that we ultimately receive from sight and insight is the gift of relationship. It is not the gift of a bigger bank account. It is not the gift of getting well. It is not the gift of cancer being cured. It is not the gift of a new job. It is not the gift of the welfare of so-and-so.

Ultimately, it is going to deal with relationships. It is going to deal with our own relationship with ourselves, with each other, and with God. That, my friends, is part of what we are in for when we are blessed with the gifts of insight and sight. Relationships are very interesting. We may think that we need no one. That we are self-contained persons. That we can stand on our own. That what we have amassed in life is something that we earned ourselves and that we have been able to pick ourselves up by our boot straps. We couldn't be further from the truth. That is total poppycock.

Another thing that happens when you and I are given this sight and insight: we begin to see things differently. For example, we begin to see people and their ways and their lives entwined in ours, and there are different things about these relationships that we didn't see before. Sometimes we become aware of the fact that justice is demanded, and our response is to realize that we need to be understanding to people who are different from us in so many ways.

While I was away on vacation, I was passing through Atlanta and I heard a speaker on the radio talking about community. He suggested that community really doesn't exist when everyone agrees on everything. When we feel safe in the presence of everyone, it's not community. Community is when we interact with those we don't understand. Community is when we are able to see people in another light in spite of our misunderstandings. So the gifts of sight and insight give us that opportunity to be able to take another look at those who are different from us.

The third benefit from this gift of sight has to do with really being able to *see*. A red cardinal on a snowbank is a wonderful sight. This past week, I was in a chair in my back yard at 6 a.m. I was thinking about the dawn as it was coming up. All of a sudden, much to my amazement, there was a shooting star. What a way to be launched into a meditation. It was a gift. And there are many gifts in our lives like that.

I have a friend who is an artist, Andrew Jauss, from Germany. I met him about thirty years ago and he was anti-everything! Anti-God, anti-church, anti-religion, anti-government, anti-parents, etc. There was nothing that Andrew could hold on to and say that he liked. It was very difficult to have a relationship with Andrew because Andrew really didn't like himself. He got into art, and he started with copying the masterpieces. This is secondhand art. Eventually he broke away and found himself. He has been on a very significant spiritual journey for a long time and I just reacquainted myself with him last year. His art is so different, but it speaks of the third element in this idea of the gifts of sight and insight, where we are able to see ordinary things just as they are.

If you had gone to the exhibit in Chicago or Columbus or Philadelphia held last year, you would see the 50-odd paintings he exhibited in this country. First of all, as you walk into the gallery, you see that they are all about 10 to 12 inches square. Secondly, they look like photographs. But they are not. They are paintings of photographs of ordinary things. The title of the exhibit is the third point of my homily: *As Things Are.* He is able to see life on life's terms, as things are.

He'll take many pictures in the course of traveling or just walking through the streets of the city. When he has developed them, he will analyze them and start to eliminate all the superfluous things that are in there. He will paint a black and white picture of what he sees. He never uses color in his paintings. He might paint a black and white picture of trash in a garbage can. Now you and I don't meditate on trash in a garbage can. That's not the point. The point is to see things as they are, not as we perceive them, not as we would like them to be, but in reality the way they are.

So, my friends, if you and I were to ask God for something today, and I presume we all have something we would like to ask God for, we have to first of all be prepared to receive it. We have to be willing to make the commitment and changes it calls for. And then, we might have to change the course of our journey.

I ask you, if God were to come to you and say, "What do you want? What can I give you?" what would be your response? Remember, when we open ourselves up, through faith, and enter into this relationship with God, we will never be the same.

Yes, it's going to cost you. Are you willing to pay for this priceless gift?

Companion on the Journey

Acts 10:34a, 37-43
Colossians 3:1-4
John 20:1-9

On behalf of the community of St. Frances of Rome, I want to welcome each and every one of you and extend to you God's choicest blessings as we gather to celebrate this great feast of Easter. It is the most important feast that we have in the Christian tradition. It is the Feast of Liberation. It is the Feast where darkness turns to light. I have been thinking that as we gather to celebrate Easter this year, we realize that there is a real similarity between what happened in the Gospel story this morning and with where we are today.

You have to remember that Jesus chose ordinary individuals and asked them to come and be part of his inner circle of friends. We know them as disciples. We know them as apostles. There were men and women. And Jesus, over a period of three years, taught these people a message that was new to them. Not simply a message about eking out an existence and putting up with the trials and tribulations of the day, with the Romans having taken over all of Judea, but he taught them a message of love. He taught them a message of forgiveness. He taught them how to love and how to be loved. He taught them how to forgive and how to be forgiven.

The disciples liked being with Jesus. They were human beings just like you and me. They were receiving something from Jesus that no one else had given them. I think we could call it *respect.* He gave them a sense of status that they never had before. Scripture tells us that they were fishermen, or tax collectors, or they had menial jobs around Capernaum. Slowly but surely Jesus gathered these people around him and they began to feel good about themselves. They began to discover a future. They began to make plans for what was going to happen in their lives. They began to dream dreams and have a vision about what their future would be with Jesus.

Interestingly enough, we know that their vision did not mesh with that of Jesus. Jesus had other things on his mind and other goals and other visions. He tried to tell them that but they didn't understand. They celebrated the ritual meal as a good Jew would. At the Passover they gathered around the table and they spoke of the Exodus. They spoke of the coming of the Messiah. They spoke of the journey of the Jew to freedom.

And then the bottom fell out of their existence. Everything started to go wrong. They met the soldiers in the olive groves in Gethsemani. Jesus was taken away. They were scared to death. They stayed on the edge and watched, or ran and hid. Jesus was put to death. Now, after his burial, they were hiding out. Tradition tells us that they were hiding out in the room where they had celebrated the Passover.

What do you think was going through their minds? What would go through your mind if you were in their position? "What am I going to do next? I have made a big mistake. Can I go back to my fishing business in Capernaum? Will they let me pay taxes at the Temple gate? What am I going to do? This man that I grew to love and understand, this man that I put all of my hopes for the future into, is dead. It is all over. What am I going to do?"

In addition to their confusion, the disciples also thought they would be captured and tortured and put to death because they were cohorts of Jesus. So they were in a very painful state of mind, to say the least.

This is no different than where you and I find ourselves many times. In the course of living life, we have dreams that are shattered. We make plans that can never be developed. We have relationships that are broken. We leave one secure experience only to find that the next one is not what we expected it to be. All of the emotional changes that happened to the disciples and apostles, we also have to face.

Just look at the papers. Watch the news. Read the front page. We are dealing with things that are out of our grasp. In our own Church we see a holy and very sick old man, the Pope. He will probably die sometime this year. We will get a new pope. And that new pope is not going to be able to answer all the questions that everyone anticipates. Some will say he is too liberal. Others will say he is too conservative. But he will be the pope.

We look at the paper and we see medical moral ethics all over the page, spoken of by doctors and theologians and ethicists and politicians, all because of a situation that few of us would want to be in. Maybe we have dealt with the life and death of an individual in the course of our experience, or maybe we are dealing with it right here and now. It is a painful experience. It is not something that we can just simply do. It has ramifications. So it is an issue.

We extend sympathy to a young woman who was married to a policeman in our community. Tomorrow, she will have to bury her husband. We extend understanding to the troubled young man, who should have been in some type of care, who pulled the trigger twice. We look at our own lives and we are facing things that we never thought we would have to face. Yet, we are facing them.

While we do have this parallel between the Old Testament and the New Testament, and the disciples and our own circumstances, there is yet another common thread. And that is our need to be in charge. We all like to be in charge. We like to have control. We want to be in control of what is going to happen to us, control of the direction our lives are going in, control over what will happen to our children, and on and on.

This is the Feast where we discover that we don't have control over anything. We really don't. If we are going to enter into the life that Christ gives to us, we have to be willing to let God be God, and we have to become the creatures that God has created out of His love. We can't take away that arrangement. We have to let God be God. And when we enter into that mindset, then, and only then, are we able to appreciate what the Resurrection is all about.

Mary Magdalene was a close friend of Jesus. She was in love with Jesus; she cared for him greatly. I hope sometime, in the next century or two, we just happen to come across a scroll of *The Gospel*

According To Mary Magdalene. Then we can understand the rest of the story! It seems to me that there is more there than what we know right now. She wanted to be there. She was dealing with her grief. She was trying to figure out what was happening. She didn't recognize Jesus when he appeared to her as the gardener. She ran up to the gardener and said, "If you have taken his body, let me know, so that I can take it and put it in a proper place." Jesus looked at her and said, "Mary." And she said, "Rabboni! (which means teacher) You are alive!" Then he said, "Don't touch me." She wanted to embrace him. She wanted to love him. She wanted to hold him. But he said, "Not yet."

That is interpreted to mean that she wanted things to be the way they used to be. And you see, my friends, life is never going to be the way it used to be. It is the way it is now, and it is the way it is going to be in the future. But we can never go back. We can never go back to the way it was at home. We can never go back to the way it was last week. We can never go back and have the same conversation we had with our friend the last time we talked to him or her.

We are in process. We are on a journey. What we learn in this resurrection experience is that we are not alone. The challenge that we have today, on the Feast of Easter, is to be able to let other people into our lives. Look at the group in this church this morning. Why are you here? Because it is Easter. Because you wanted to come here. But the diversity of the people in this church is amazing! You all bring your different gifts, your different outlooks, your different opinions. And it all comes together. When it does, as in a great centrifuge, then we find something to give to each other that sustains us as we continue the journey. That's what we call the Incarnation of Christ. That's what we call Jesus Christ.

In lieu of being part of a community where we support each other and know each other and continue our journey as Christians united, we look for distractions. We look for a place to go or we dream about a trip. I told the people last night that I was so glad that U of L won that I didn't know what to do! At least, for a moment, there was a distraction — distraction from the war and from all the other things we have to deal with. If you think about it, we do *create* distractions, don't we? Then, we don't have to deal with the really painful side of living. Because we are afraid that if we do deal with that painful side of living, we will have to do it on our own.

The message of the gospel today is that *we don't deal with it on our own*. We deal with it with the love of God and the grace of the Spirit that is given to us.

Today, as you celebrate Easter, set aside all of the distractions and allow yourself to realize that you are loved as you are, not in a state of perfection, but as a human being, dealing with whatever you are dealing with. Ask for the help to be able to continue to walk through life with God. God has many faces and many eyes and many arms and many feet. And God is found in this community.

Catholic with a Small *c*

Isaiah 56:1, 6-7
Romans 11:13-15. 29-32
Matthew 15:21-28

If you look at the three readings we have for today, there is a central theme that is quite obvious. The theme is that of universality. This is one of the marks of the Church. Universal means catholic, with a small "*c*". In our first reading, we find the Prophet Isaiah speaking to the people about the family of God. This is a new theme in the Book of Isaiah that speaks of all people being part of the extended family of God. Isaiah says that we are all invited into the House of God, which is our house of prayer.

This is a new approach because before the time of Isaiah, we found a lot of division. We found one fighting against another. We found differences in languages as well as in beliefs. Now we find this theme that starts to bring us together as God's creation, from one who witnesses to the belief in God and is given to charity and respect for others. We are told that Isaiah lived some six hundred years before the Christian era.

We listen to the second reading, and find that Paul, who is Jewish but yet a Roman by citizenship, was called by God to be the Apostle of the Gentiles. Paul has left the family chosen by God as the family from which Christianity would develop. He has gone to the Gentiles. Paul tells the Gentiles that they, indeed, are part of God's family. He announces that as part of God's family, they have a relationship with others. And that it is incumbent upon everyone to be able to eliminate or break down the prejudices and the walls that keep us from being part of God's family. Paul says that God forgives us readily. That God gives us freedom. That God loves us beyond our comprehension.

Then we look at the Gospel today. It is a different kind of Gospel. I think that it is appropriate to say that Jesus is trying to teach his people, this very prejudiced community, a lesson by role playing. Think about it. Jesus and his friends have gone through the region of Tyre and Sidon. This area was looked down upon. It wasn't one of the more respected regions of Israel.

A Canaanite woman, similar to a Samaritan woman, has a sick child. So she comes to Jesus and begs him to heal her daughter. But Jesus ignores her. Now certainly this is out of character for Jesus. And the disciples come and say, "Let's get rid of this woman. She keeps calling after us. She is bothering us!" (Sounds like something that you or I would say if we are irritated by someone.) Jesus says no. Then he has an insulting dialogue with the woman. He says, "It is not right for me to give good things to someone who doesn't believe."

The woman replies, "But, after all, the dogs do eat the crumbs that fall from the table of the master." Jesus tests her to the point where he embraces her. And he lifts her up and he says, "You have such great faith." In this particular passage, I like to imagine her begging on her knees, on the ground beneath Jesus. And Jesus picks her up and he hugs her and says, "Go home. Your daughter is going to get well."

This is a very important scene for us. When you and I start to talk about universality, and we are talking about the catholic oneness of all those who believe in Jesus Christ, we can automatically fall back on our own prejudices that separate us from others. We can read things in our newspaper and in journals and find enough excuses to point our fingers at other people.

But we can't afford as Catholic people, with a capital "C", to point our fingers at anyone. We have enough issues to take care of ourselves right here and now. You and I are not free from our biases and opinions. Quite the contrary. We hold on to them tenaciously.

There are people that are often referred to as fringe people, who hesitate to come into the community or to the House of God because they don't feel accepted. They don't feel worthy. The Church has come out with statements of their unworthiness. And we have allowed that to happen and we believe it. Think about the addicts. Think about people with different sexual orientation. Think about all kinds of "socially unacceptable" individuals. Then we have to ask ourselves what we need to do to make these people wanted and part of the people of the House of God.

It is up to you and me to do this. Just as the theology and insights about God's relationship with us have gradually evolved over a period of centuries to the present time, I can guarantee you that in years to come, the attitudes that you and I hold today will change. I have no doubt that there will be women priests. I have no doubt that there will be married clergy. I have no doubt that the whole construct of the Church will evolve into something different from what we are used to here and now.

But sometimes we hold on tenaciously to defend our position. When we do this, we close our minds and our hearts to each other. Yet, we call ourselves catholic, with a small *"c"*.

We can't afford to do that. We are challenged, as Isaiah and Paul and Jesus challenged their people. So I challenge you, and I challenge myself at the same time, to be open. Open to everyone. We have to embrace each other as people who are in the process of becoming.

That's who we are: people in the process of becoming the ultimate friend of God, blessed beyond our imagination, beyond our grasp. We live out our lives each day, humbly and quietly, but with an open mind and an open spirit, and with a prayer to be able to understand someone else. And we never close our door to anyone who comes and wants to be part of our community.

That's the challenge. That's who we really are. The word "catholic" didn't come into existence until the second century by a man named Ignatius of Antioch. He talked about the whole human race, the whole relationship that we have with each other. How are the needed changes going to take place? How have such changes taken place in the past?

You know, there are two ways of looking at authority. We have people in authority telling us what to do. It happens, and then we get upset about it. Or, we have authority coming from the grassroots, which naturally evolves, and then we are more likely to embrace the changes and new concepts.

It is not an easy task to be part of the universal family of God. But it is our task. It is our task to reach out and embrace each other. And not to just simply ignore people because they are different or they have a different opinion than we do. We can never be that sure of our own position, can we? The louder we protest, the more insecure we are.

Today, we have a good lesson to take home with us. It is a lesson of universality. It is a lesson of love. It is a lesson of forgiveness. It is a lesson of embracing all people and inviting them to be part of God's house of prayer.

We Don't Need a Lot of Stuff

Amos 7:12-15
Mark 6:7-13

When we take the opportunity to investigate the main characters of the Old and New Testaments we will find out that, with the exception of Isaiah and Ezekiel, the prophets were not trained for the tasks they assumed. Quite the contrary. They were just ordinary people doing ordinary things in the experience of life as they found it in their day. The same is true for the apostles, the disciples and all the rest.

Perhaps the same is true with you and me. However, one of the things that happens to us is that we reach a certain plateau. In reaching this plateau, we tend to sort of cool it! We tend to maintain. We just maintain where we are and live our lives in a rather ordinary way. The people of the Old Testament maintained. The apostles initially maintained. The disciples maintained. And you and I maintain.

What happens when we maintain? Nothing. We just simply exist. We get up. We do our tasks. We go to bed. We get up. We do our tasks. We go to bed. When we don't break out of the sense of maintaining, then life is not really exciting for us. Not only is life not exciting, but nothing really creative starts to happen. Nothing moves our creative juices. We don't have vision, in other words, to look at things in a different way.

In the readings today, you and I are challenged to leave the posture of maintaining and to realize that we have been given everything we need to be able to go beyond the moment of simply existing and to be able to make a contribution.

This past week, I think it was the Louisville Forum who

met to discuss a problem in our community. The problem centered around the lack of money and finances for the Louisville Orchestra. They gathered together some significant individuals in our community who are capable of making changes. They invited someone from outside who is an authority on the cultural scene of the nation. They discussed what they could do to meet the needs of more endowments for the orchestra and to be able to sustain them. As we have experienced their presence in our community for years, we do not want it to fail.

The man from the outside came in and he challenged the group. He said, "You don't want to simply maintain the Louisville Orchestra. When you are in this position, as you are here in this community, now is not the time to wring your hands. Now is the time to make a major investment into what the Louisville Orchestra can become, not just for us, but for the whole nation, for the world. But remember, if you will, the history of the orchestra. The Louisville Orchestra was world-known because it was the premier orchestra for new works that were being developed by many artists. The new recordings were made by your orchestra. You don't have to wring your hands. You have to go ahead and look and dream about what this orchestra can become throughout the entire world."

Well, this really set the locals back a bit! They said, "But how can we do this?" The speaker said, "You have to have a vision! You have to have a vision of what this orchestra can become and then you have to create it." Someone tried to be practical and said, "Wouldn't it be better if we tried to reduce the number of musicians in the orchestra from 75 to 50?" And the speaker said, "Absolutely not. You can't afford to reduce the number of your musicians. If you do that, you don't have the ability to play Bach or Beethoven or the classics that people come to hear. You need to create a whole new concept or image of the orchestra that will bring people here in droves!"

What he was saying is exactly what the scriptures are saying today. We can't simply exist, wring our hands and say "What are we going to do? Isn't this a terrible experience?" We have to look at the opportunities. We have to be able to dream the dreams and start to put them into position. When we do that, wonderful things start to happen.

I remember being absolutely delighted when I heard that Fr. Tim Hogan had been named pastor at St. Boniface Church on Liberty. St. Boniface was a good Franciscan parish, but the Order could no longer keep the place going. Tim Hogan is a man of vision. He has always said, "How can I make this a better experience," whether at Catholic Charities or now as a pastor. Now he is opening a school. And people are saying, "Why is he opening that school? There aren't any kids down there." The kids will come. It is a brand new school. It is a visionary type of school, in session 12 months a year, with a lot of individual tutoring, a new type of school for the city of Louisville.

Just watch it! It is going to become a wonderful experience for the people in that area! And I can guarantee you this. St. Boniface is going to come more alive and become a great parish. Why? Because one man has come and experienced a situation, analyzed it and developed a vision. And that vision is going to come true, I guarantee it.

That is what you and I ought to do. We are not to be wringing our hands and saying "Aren't things terrible?" For the last 18 to 20 months the Church in this archdiocese has gone through a terribly painful stage. You hear people saying, "It's terrible." "What should we do?" "The place is falling apart." "Maybe I'll relocate." "The church on the corner might be better." "The Baptist Church is not bad either." "Maybe I'll go out to Southeast Christian." "Maybe I'll go to the Episcopalians. They're almost like us. Maybe I'll find something there."

People are thinking such things. I've got news for you. They don't want these people. They would be taking the same inactivity and the same lack of commitment to God and simply putting it someplace else. They would go there for a while and then end up searching again.

That's the challenge of the Gospel today. Amos didn't want to be a prophet. He was very happy being a shepherd, and he liked to travel around. He was a nomad. God came along and said, "You are going to be a prophet." "But I don't want to be a prophet," Amos said. God said, "Amos, get out of your selfishness and start dreaming dreams. Find your purpose in life. Find out what you can do for others." "But I have no education," Amos replied. "I have no background."

People today say that also: "I haven't read the entire Bible." "I haven't gone to college." "I've never been to the seminary." You don't have to be a scholar. You know what your greatest asset in dealing with another individual is? Your way of dealing with human experience. It's as you and I deal with human experience on the journey of life that we are able to add authenticity to our lives. And that's what makes it possible for someone else to say "That individual did it this way. Maybe I can too."

In the gospel today Jesus said, "Don't travel with a lot of stuff." We don't need a lot of stuff. We don't need the degree. We don't need the trappings of importance. We have enough in ourselves to deal with life on life's terms. If we find that there is great value within ourselves as we experience life, then we are prompted to get out of this malaise of simply maintaining. We are able to dream dreams. We are able to make a difference in our lives and in the lives of others.

I'll share this with you this morning. I've set a goal for myself. This is something I want to do. Some years ago I found out that in the medieval days there were great pilgrimages from places in France like Toulouse over to great cathedrals in Spain, like Santiago de Compostela. I have always been fascinated with this. People would spend months walking the walk all the way from France to Spain.

Then I came across five people here in Louisville who have made this pilgrimage. Businessmen who have taken the time to go and walk. It is not only a physical experience but it is also a spiritual experience. So I found a map of this route and I had it framed. Three weeks ago the *New York Times*, in the travel section, published an article on making this particular trip. That was all I needed. That was the form of confirmation I needed! So I have decided that when I am 70 years old, I am going to make the trip.

It is not important whether I make the trip or not. What is important is that I am dreaming about the trip. I'm reading about the trip. I am willing to enter into the possibility of taking two months of time and going across and visiting the cathedral. Why? Because I want to. That is the only reason you have to have: just because you want to. If anybody cares to go along, fine.

So, I suggest this morning that we ponder: do we want to simply exist, maintain, wring our hands, and look for an acceptable option in the generic system, which doesn't exist, or do we want to be able to reflect that we have everything we need to find our own vision. A vision that would make it possible for us to get out of our ruts, and really get into what Christ is calling us to do. Think you can do it? Sure you can. All you have to do is to *want to*. You've got everything else you need.

The Gift of Scripture

Luke 10:25-37

It has long been a tradition of our ritual to read Sacred Scripture, at least three segments of it, in the first part of our Liturgy. We usually read a passage each from the Old and the New Testament, and a reading from one of the four Gospels. Sacred Scripture is a very important part of our tradition. It is indeed the cornerstone of the story of Christ and of Christianity. It is a living part of our tradition; it has the opportunity to feed our spiritual beings, to give us insights into ordinary experiences that we might be facing here and now.

Too many times over the years, though, I think that we have sterilized scripture. By this I mean that we have taken away the real meaning of scripture; the passion, the story, the personalities of the individuals we read about. They just become a name and a figure to us. We haven't dealt with the customs and the rites of the day in which the passages were written. Often, we don't know the meaning behind certain verses and passages. We also don't really appreciate the parables, or stories. The gospel today is a parable. It didn't really happen. It was a story that Jesus used to teach a message.

There are also parables in the Old Testament. They are not necessarily as well defined as they are in the New Testament. Yet, they are stories passed on by word of mouth, which taught about an aspect of the relationship between God and His people. So today, I suggest that we start to revisit and try to understand scripture as scripture.

Scripture is not dull. Quite the contrary! If you get into it and start to pick it apart and look at the manner and the customs of the time, it becomes rather exciting. And I can assure you that in the whole of the bible, every aspect of life is covered.

This morning we have a story. The story is introduced by the question of a lawyer saying to Jesus the Teacher: "Which is the greatest of the commandments? What do I need to do to be saved?" he asked. Now, why did he ask that question? It is important for us to know that there were five or six hundred laws that had been mentioned by various teachers as necessary for salvation. So Jesus' reply was not original to him. He said, "Love God and your neighbor as yourself." That is known as the *Shama*. It is an ancient concept of law. So Jesus reached back into his experience and brought forth an ancient statement that summed all of the laws up. He just simply said, "What does the law say? It says "Love God, your neighbor and yourself."

But then, to justify himself, the lawyer said, "But who is my neighbor?" Now, for that time, this was a good question. If we ask ourselves what that means, we would say that everyone is our neighbor: the people who live on our street, the people we work with, the people we deal with in stores, our community here at church, etc. This was not so at the time of Jesus. At that time, the neighbor was the one that you would share your first name with. The neighbor was the one who lived in your town or who shared the same beliefs.

So Jesus told a story. He told about a man who traveled the road from Jerusalem to Jericho. These were two powerful and commercial cities. Along that route, caravans would travel. Travelers were constantly being waylaid, ambushed, robbed and killed. It was a treacherous road to travel. People would never travel it by themselves. They would always go in a group.

When Jesus said, "The man went down from Jerusalem to Jericho," his disciples knew that the man was doing something very foolish. They knew that he had put himself in grave danger. You and I wouldn't ordinarily know that. We would just think it was as if he was going from here to Bardstown. Then Jesus added that the man fell in with robbers who left him half dead. The story goes on to say that a priest came along and found the individual, but he passed him by. The disciples knew the priest did this because of the law of contamination. If the man was dead, the priest would've had to go through a great ritual of purification.

It was a logical act. The disciples had no issue with this.

They knew exactly why the priest went on. You and I may say that he just didn't want to get involved. The same was true of the Levite. The Levites were the priestly family of the tribes. From the tribe of Levi came the priests who worshiped in the Temple. They could not become involved in such an experience either because of the law of contamination. So the Levite passed the broken man by.

Then came the Samaritan. The Samaritan was a half-breed, one who didn't appreciate the strict observance of the Jewish law. The Samaritans had their own town. They were ridiculed by the orthodox Jews, who would not trade with them or visit with them or pass through their town. The Samaritans were anathema, as we would say. But it was this man, this man who was ridiculed by the orthodox Jew, who came to the rescue of the poor man who fell in with robbers.

The lesson that Jesus was trying to instill in the disciples was the fact that there are times when we have to overlook our prejudices and our differences and minister to each other. Therein we find the opportunity to serve. You could probably sum it up by saying that "actions speak louder than words."

But it brings up the point that you and I really need to take the opportunity to delve into scripture and to find the actual meaning of passages. Unfortunately, we haven't had that opportunity, especially as Catholics. Around 1900, the Church said that we shouldn't read scripture because we might misinterpret it. So we had bible story books instead. Remember them? They were clean translations of what we needed to know about Abraham, Isaac, Jacob and the Old Testament characters. For many of us, that is our frame of reference when it comes to understanding scripture. Unfortunately, we haven't been blessed with the opportunity to really experience the depth of the knowledge that has been given to us by our scripture scholars and by the sciences such as anthropology and archeology. There is a rich treasure of opportunity for us to really examine scripture and to be able to understand the meaning and the message that's given to us in scripture. It is not simply dead words.

Some years ago I went to St. Meinrad for a private retreat. I had a retreat master whom I met with once a day for an hour. He was a scripture scholar. He gave me a book from the New Testament to read. He told me that we would meet each day and talk about what I had found in the book. He said he would be asking me how God was speaking to me through the gospel. I decided that I would approach the book as if it was a script for a play. So I defined all the characters in the book. I would ask myself such questions as "What did Mary look like? What did Joseph look like? What did their house look like?" Then I would write descriptions of each of the disciples and the stories, etc. I felt good about it. It was sort of a novel way to get into studying the book.

After a couple of days I met with the Retreat Master. I told him about the play of Matthew according to Jerry Eifler. We were going along through the chapters when he stopped and said, "You have left something out! You haven't talked about the Sower of the Seed? Why did you leave that out?" I said, "Well, it didn't mean too much to me. Sowing a seed is sowing a seed." Then he said, "But you have missed the whole message of the book by not dealing with the sower. Do you know how they sowed the seed?" I said, "I guess not. How?" He went on to say that they would take a forked stick and go out onto the hillside and they would scratch the ground a little bit. They wouldn't till it or manure it. They didn't do anything except scratch the ground. Then they would take their garment and make a pocket where they would put the seed. They would take some seed and broadcast it up in the air where it would then fall to the ground. That was the way the seed was sown.

The retreat master reiterated that this was all they did. He told me that they didn't even have to water it. He then asked me, "Do you understand the message?" When I shook my head "no" he went on to say that all we have to do is what we have to do. We don't have to complicate life. We simply prepare the ground the best we can and then *we let God take over*. God is the One who waters and germinates and brings the sun and produces the fruit and takes care of the harvest. He then told me that the meaning of the book that I was studying is that God is with us always. And you know what? He was right! And one of the reasons why I missed the point was because I didn't know the customs of the time.

So today, I encourage you to take the time to listen to the scriptures. Take the time to pick up a commentary from one of the book stores. They give us a rich insight into what is really being spoken to us. When we do this, the Word comes alive. Then we have something to take home.

When the question is asked as it is in the gospel today, "Who is my neighbor?" we can ask back, "Who can I be a neighbor to?" When I was reflecting on this gospel, I put myself in the position of the man who had fallen in a heap and was unconscious. I was eventually in an inn and suddenly woke up. How would I feel if the person who came to my rescue was a person I didn't like? I would have to make a quick change if the person who saved my life was a person I had ignored or minimized, wouldn't I? I spent a bit of time thinking about this. We never know who this neighbor is. Sure, it might be our best friend. But it could also be the person who was getting under our skin. Here they are now, loving us and nursing us back to health.

Yes, scripture has a wealth of gifts to give to us. We are the ones who need to scratch the ground to be able to discover the seed, the voice of God, and to make it our own. And to always remember that actions speak louder than words.

Water for the Road

Romans 5:1-2.5-8
John 4:5-42

As I have mentioned before, our liturgical calendar is stretched over three years. As we began our liturgical year at the beginning of Advent in December, we started with Cycle A. We will commence Cycle B next Advent, and then follow the next year with Cycle C. When it comes to Lent, and mid-Lent more specifically, we have individuals who speak for a mystery in various ways. This Sunday we have the woman at the well, a Samaritan, a half-breed who is looked down upon by the Orthodox Jew. Next Sunday, we will have the blind man, who searches out someone to give him the gift of sight. Then the following Sunday, we will have the story of Lazarus, who was brought back from the dead.

Our liturgy is so constructed over a period of these three years that it gives us a tremendous amount of theology and insight into the mystery of Incarnation, the mystery of Salvation, and the mystery of Redemption. To appreciate this, we have to be aware of the ordinary things that are used in our scripture. And at this point, we are talking about the element of water.

I guess Bahrain may be the driest place on the planet. To get water in Bahrain, divers have to go down with a large rock to underground springs that are deep in the sea, and catch fresh water in a skin, and bring it up to provide water for the people who live there. It is a desperate experience to be without water. We have all been thirsty, but to be without water to sustain our cattle, or the lives of our loved ones, is something else. We know this from the practical standpoint. From the spiritual standpoint, we see water as the life-giving element in Baptism.

We see water spoken of in the creation of the world. When God created the great Sea, he blew his breath over the water to bring life to all. We see water referred to in the Exodus, when Moses took the people out of Egypt, out of bondage, and took them into the desert. They were blessed with water. Water, then, becomes not only a symbol of life, but also a blessing. We see Noah and the Ark, and the great waters that flooded the earth to cleanse it again, so that the act of Redemption could take place.

In the story that we have for our Gospel today, we see the well of Jacob. You may remember that Jacob was blind. Jacob had a young son who was named Joseph, who was sold into bondage and became the head of the Egyptian organization. His brothers were desperate so they had to go and beg for freedom. As a sign of blessing, Jacob gave to Joseph a cistern, a source of water that would sustain his flock, his people, and would provide for all of their needs, not only physically, but also spiritually.

So we have this setting in our reading today: Jacob's well, used for centuries by many people coming to Samaria. There is a problem, however. The problem has to do with Samaria itself because the Samaritans are half-breeds. They are a group of people who were basically Jewish, who got involved and married into a pagan culture or into another tribe, diminishing the purity of the Jewish race. The Orthodox Jews would never have anything to do with the Samaritans. They would just simply ignore them. They certainly did not want to become contaminated by them.

In today's story, Jesus decided to go to the Samaritan town with his disciples. Jesus was going to stay out at the well while the disciples went into town for supplies. He met this woman, who by the way, has a name. Her name is Photeine, a very ancient name. She was considered a saint in the third, fourth and fifth centuries by the Greek Orthodox Church and by other Christian denominations around the Mediterranean.

Photeine was sitting there. I think for an appreciation of what is going to happen, you have to give yourself an opportunity to let your mind freely associate and come up with the type of person

Photeine really is, given the information we have. She has been married five times and she is living with a guy who is not her husband. She is a rather forceful person in the community. When she speaks, people listen. She is thirsty. She has gone to this "blankety-blank" well one more time. So she is sitting there. I don't think she is a happy woman. She is frustrated with life in many different ways. So this Jew, Jesus, comes along and says, "Give me a drink."

The woman fires right back at him and says, "Why are you, a Jew, asking me for a drink? What is wrong with you? You've got no business asking me for a drink! I might contaminate you!" Jesus says, "But I need a drink." What we don't realize is that Jesus is extending to her an invitation. A very special invitation to fulfill something she has longed for her entire life.

What is it that she has longed for her entire life? To answer that question just simply ask yourself, what have you been looking for your entire life? What is it that you really want? What will give you that sense of peace, of fulfillment, that Paul speaks of in the second reading this morning? So when Jesus comes along and says, "Give me a drink," he is speaking figuratively. Whether he needed a drink or not doesn't really matter. When he was giving her the invitation to respond to him, he went on a little further and said, "If you really realized who was asking you for a drink, you would know that I can give you the living water to care for all your needs the rest of your life." Then she says, "Give me that! I like that! I need that!"

Jesus replies," But you have to give me a drink." So they get into this business of the water. It gets a little muddy at this point because she is only on a practical level and Jesus is on a spiritual level. Jesus challenges her by saying, "Go tell your husband to come." She replies, "I have no husband." Jesus said, "You are right. You have been married five times and the man you are living with now is not your husband." Then the woman exclaimed, "Indeed, you are a prophet."

Then Photeine starts talking about herself from a spiritual standpoint. She says, "I know that there is a Messiah who is promised to us. And I know that there is a Christ who is promised to us. When he comes, that Christ is going to fill us with all that we need. But in the meantime, here I am at the well of Jacob."

What this woman is doing is responding to the invitation

of faith. You really wouldn't expect this woman to have a deep appreciation for the traditions of Judaism. But she does. Not only does she have it, but she is willing to share it with this stranger. Now you have a manifestation of faith. You have a woman who has paid a high price for love, who has gone to the *nth* degree to have her needs satisfied. She has set all of this aside and now she is talking to this Jewish rabbi about redemption.

With that, she leaves. She runs off to the town and she tells the people in the town, "You have to come and listen to this guy I just met. You won't believe what he has told me. He has told me everything about myself. And it doesn't matter. I am still acceptable. All the things that you know I have done, that have scandalized you, really don't matter to this man. He still gives me this great gift."

So they all come out to see who this guy is. Initially they say, "We came out to see you because of her words." But after he stayed with them for two days, they said, "We don't believe because of her words anymore. We believe because of your actions: the way you treated us; the way you have opened your heart to us, not just to the saved Jew, but also to us Samaritans, who were minimized, who had broken all of the rules of Moses. And you have accepted us also."

So you have, then, a change of heart. You have the first sign of conversion as spoken of in the New Testament in a dramatic way. That's why, according to the legends of Origen, of St. Augustine and some of the early writers, that this woman is held in such high esteem. She was able to receive the gift, and understand the gift that Jesus was giving to her. The gift of living water, of constant grace. The gift of the ability to continue her journey, and to let bygones be bygones.

Her sins were forgiven. She had a change of status. In the very early writings of the Fathers of the Church, we find that she was considered an apostle, believe it or not. She was canonized by the Greek and Russian Churches. She was also supposed to have left Samaria and gone off to Carthage in Africa where she was imprisoned for the faith and died a martyr. She was said to have converted Nero's daughter and a hundred of her slaves.

There are a lot of legends about our friend at the well. But the real meaning of the gospel has nothing to do with all of these incidentals of the story. What it has to do with is the need that Jesus had to share faith. She was the first recipient of that faith. She received the gift of life that sustained her forever on the rest of her journey.

Where does this leave us today? It leaves us in the position where it is all ours for the taking. All we have to do is let go and let God. We will receive the gift, and never be thirsty again, be filled forever. That is what redemption is all about. That is the ultimate gift of Baptism.

New Day Dawning

Galatians 4:4-7
Luke 2:16-21

Good morning and Happy New Year to you. This is absolutely an energizing day for me. I always look forward to New Year's Day. It is an opportunity to establish a benchmark in the course of living. New Year's Eve, for me, is a quiet time when I like to be by myself. I think and write down some things I want to remember as the year ends. Then, in the morning, there is the beginning of a new day and a new year. This morning, I got up and went through the usual rituals, and then got in my car and went out to find the buddies I drink coffee with. Over the rooftops I saw one of the most magnificent sunrises I have ever seen! It was the new day dawning in great splendor. That's the way I like to approach the New Year, with the opportunity of a new day dawning.

It's very similar to the Gospel we read this morning. It was a new day dawning for them too, when they discovered that what the angels had told them was true in the small Nativity scene in Bethlehem. You have to remember that these shepherds were the lowest of the low on the social ladder in their lifetime. They certainly weren't respected. Some even considered them to be thieves. Tolerated at best, they didn't really enjoy a good reputation.

The interesting thing about this gospel of Luke is that he focuses on these people in the beginning of the story. This sense of the poor or the outcast is found all through the writings of Luke. We also find Jesus, Mary and Joseph, a poor family, away from their home and dependent upon the goodness of others.

I think that the revelation of God to the shepherds is a very strong symbol for us as we celebrate the New Year and this Feast of Mary. In the Greek church, there are two major icons. One is the icon of Christ, who holds the book and extends the blessing. The other is of Mary called the *Theotokos*, which means Christ Bearer. It was Mary's role as the conduit of God to all people, through the birth of Jesus, that gave her the dignity that she has in the Greek church as well as in the Roman church.

That's what we celebrate today: the fact of Mary being the conduit, the instrument, the way, that is spoken of in the second reading. God chose that time to bring a sense of security, salvation and dignity to His people. So the first people to receive that gift were the poor, the shepherds, Mary and Joseph—then ultimately, you and me.

This past year hasn't been the best of years—for me, anyway. We've had to face a lot of things in our diocese. We've questioned a lot of things about our church, to say nothing about the wars and the other world events. Yet, we are given the opportunity to hope.

This sense of hope and well-being comes when you and I can become a conduit for God to work within this world. That is our function. That's what we are about, when we set our own agendas aside, and we open our minds and our hearts and let God speak to us. Just as it happened with Mary, it happened with the apostles, as it happened with the shepherds. All of these people, in their own way, stepped aside and let God come and work through them. That's our function. That's what we are charged to do as Christian people. That's our past. And the result of that past is a sense of well-being. It is a sense of hope. It is a sense of realizing that regardless of what happens in our world, in our own personal lives, in our communities, that we'll be okay. We know that God is with us. We know that we need not fear the unknown or the suspicious events of the day. We have the opportunity to be gifted with hope.

I think *that* is what we celebrate. That is what I hold on to today. It is a new day, a new beginning. It might not be the best day, or the warmest day, or the day that fulfills all of our expectations. But then, what day ever does? There is no perfect day, but the security that we have in realizing that we have been blessed by God, and that

Mary, as the Christ Bearer, gives us the challenge to continue.

So I hope you accept that challenge. I hope this new day is a blessed day for you. We look forward to the day this year when we can be instruments of peace and love and forgiveness for others around us.

And I hope we can gather again next year on New Year's Day, and share the opportunities we were given this new year to help others, and to realize that we are part of God's plan.

Take the Risk to Be Happy

Acts 1:1-11
Eph 4:1-13
Mk 16:15-20

We celebrate the Feast of the Ascension of Our Lord on Sunday instead of on Thursday this year. It has been transferred by the Church. When we reflect upon this feast, we discover that there are a few different versions of the feast. It you look at the gospels you will find that the evangelists don't treat it to the extent that Luke does in the Acts of the Apostles. Actually, the Ascension has taken place in some fashion according to the evangelists, and the last scene is of Mary Magdalene going back to the place where the disciples are in hiding. This completes the whole circle of Christ's ministry, from the Nativity to the Ascension.

If we read the gospels, we find out that there is still that element of fear within the infant community of Jesus, which was mainly the disciples and apostles. They are not quite sure what is going on. Then we look at Luke's work in the Acts of the Apostles and we find out that when he talks about Jesus being taken into heaven, and the disciples can't figure out what has happened, there is a significant amount of doubt present. "How can this be? What is happening?"

So we have two elements to keep in mind this morning as we consider the Feast of the Ascension. One is fear. The second is doubt.

When we consider an event like the Ascension, or any singular event in our lives, we many times have the feeling of either fear or doubt. It might manifest itself in such a way that our approach is "I'm not sure if I want to become involved in this or not" or "I think I'll wait and see how this is going to work out." And that was certainly part of the mindset of the Church, because they thought that Jesus would return almost immediately and take them to the place that he had prepared. So, logically they said to themselves, "Why should we worry about the future since we are not going to be here that long?"

When we reflect on these responses, "Wait and see" and "I don't think I want to get involved," we discover this is often the way we do things in our lives. If that is the case, then our life does not develop. Not only our physical life, but our spiritual and our emotional lives don't develop either. What we are challenged with on this feast is to get to work. Just as the angels looked at the disciples and said, "Why are you looking up to us? Why don't you get on with the program?"

That's what we are challenged to do as Christian people. We are not invited simply to be idle spectators at events like the Eucharist. We are to be involved in this Eucharist. Being involved means that we have to risk a little. We have to allow the last part of today's Gospel to really sink into our very beings. Where Jesus said to his disciples, even in their doubts, "I am with you to the end of the age." Now if God is with us to the very end, then you and I will complete the reality of life in a very safe posture. But it doesn't just happen. We have to take action.

When I was ordained in 1961, I had an excellent mentor. I was sent to Our Mother of Sorrows parish and the pastor was a wise man who taught me a lot of things. One thing that particularly sticks out in my mind was when he walked into my office one day and said, "My boy, what you really need is a hobby." I said, "Why is a hobby such a big deal?" He answered, "You have to find balance in your life. You can't put all of your emotional eggs in one basket. You have to have appropriate outlets."

He came in another day and said, "My boy, you need to travel!" I'm sure Father John Lyons is looking down with a great smile on his face this morning, saying, "He listened to what I had to say!" Travel gives us the opportunity to expand our horizons, to be aware of other peoples and other cultures. This helps us to see that we don't have all the answers. It is important for us to have a wide experience in life. But to do this we have to take risks. You and I both know that if we are going to wait and see if it works out, nothing will ever happen. We are simply just going to exist in a very small world, whether it be our spiritual, physical or emotional world.

Somehow if we are challenged to do things, to dream dreams, to put dreams into actions, to get involved, our lives are going to be rich and full. And there is no age limit when it comes to doing new things in life. There is sometimes doubt, there are risks, but there are no rules to be broken.

I met a woman some years ago in another parish. Her name was Edna Finn—a delightful lady. She kept a meticulous house. She was married to Henry Finn, who was an attorney. They had no children. Henry was interested in dabbling in art. He would paint and he would draw and he bought lots of supplies for his hobby. Periodically, Edna would walk in and say, "Oh, Henry, clean up your mess. Put all that stuff away." Eventually, Henry died. Edna gathered together all of his art supplies. She thought to herself, "What did he see in all of this? What did he get out of painting pictures?"

Such questions prompted her to sit down one day and start fooling around with the paintbrush. Soon she began to discover something about herself. She got involved. And she got so involved that I don't think she ever cleaned her house again. It made a tremendous difference in this woman's life. Over a period of time, she discovered a whole new circle of friends. She was recognized for her art and her talents. She was known as Louisville's "Grandma Moses." Two of her paintings were printed on the front of *The Louisville Magazine*. She lived to a ripe old age. She always invited people into her life. A stranger who could paint was welcomed into her home.

She took us on trips for the day, down to Breckenridge County or to places around Louisville, and we would just have a conversation and then paint. It really didn't matter if we finished the painting. It didn't matter if we created a masterpiece or made a total disaster. That wasn't the issue at all. The issue was that we were communicating with each other and sharing ideas.

Edna, in her ordinary way, was carrying out the mission that Jesus gave to his disciples. She lived out her Christian life, her Christian beliefs by just simply being the person she was. Edna found the zest for living. She took the risks. She experienced life. She was a very happy woman. And she was truly a gift to our community.

Just this week I came across an eighty-year-old gentleman who is just starting to take violin lessons. And why is he taking violin lessons? Because he wants to! He said, "I've always wanted to play the violin, and I'm going to do it before I die."

I know another gentleman who just recently started taking piano lessons. It is not too late. Enter into the risk. Don't stand there and say, "When I have time, I'm going to take lessons."

"When I have time I am going to do it." That's like the guy who always said that when he retired, he was going to get a fishing boat and go fishing on the lake. He retired. He never bought the boat. All his expectations about how he was going to handle his retirement never happened. Because it has to happen *now*. It must happen *before* we have that extra time.

The message of the Ascension is precisely about this—about taking the opportunity to continue our growth. To be happy people. To take a risk with the confidence that we will be okay. When we do that our life becomes full. Then we really witness a belief in the life of Jesus Christ in so many different ways. We don't have to take on a religious habit or go to a monastery. Quite the contrary. All we have to do is simply live up to our potential—the potential that we see for ourselves, not the expectations of other people. It really doesn't matter what we do as long as we find a sense of satisfaction in doing it. When we do, then the mission of Christ continues.

So the challenge is simply to be open. To risk. To set aside that argument of fear. To be able to think about "what I would really like to do."

I don't know when this happened to me but it happened. I decided that I really hoped that when I die, I die with no regrets. The things that I might end up doing might be disasters to other people. But at least I have done it. We don't have to be stuck in a fixed position for the rest of our lives.

In conclusion, it is interesting to note that studies have told us, and it has been borne out, that if a priest has not developed a hobby or any outside interests, when he retires and is taken out of his affirming environment, the probability is that he will die within eighteen months. It happens too often, simply because he has nothing to do. He doesn't have another life. He is very narrow. He has lived a safe life.

Maybe the same can be said for many of you as well. Jesus came to bring to us the opportunity to live life to its fullest. But it still remains that you and I have to dream the dream, have the desire and take the step. When we do, a whole new vista of life, friends and blessings open before us.

Candy Wrapper Advice

1 Samuel 3:3b-10, 19
1 Corinthians 6:13-15, 17-20
John 1:35-42

I was on retreat last weekend. It was a good retreat. After we had the opening prayer and dinner, they passed out candy. So I took a couple of pieces and stuffed them in my pocket. It was Dove candy. Later on in the evening I was walking along and I felt the candy in my pocket. I took it out and when I unwrapped it, there was a message inside. I read the message and thought, "Isn't this something?" The message was this: *Push yourself to notice the extraordinary in the ordinary.* I thought, "That is a good theme for a retreat!"

So that sort of set my pace for the retreat. During the conferences that we had and the talks and the conversations, I sort of let that phrase ruminate in my mind. Take the ordinary things that we do and find the extraordinary in them. You would be surprised at what you can see. There are so many things that we take for granted. So many things have always been there and have always been part of our surroundings, and we don't take the opportunity to really appreciate what unique gifts have been given to us.

The next morning, after breakfast, I discovered that I still had the other piece of candy. I took it from my pocket, opened it, and read: *The reward for a good deed is to have done it.* There is a lot to ponder in that statement also! So many times we expect something in return. We expect a compensation of some sort. Either a compliment or a word of praise or a pat on the back or even a feeling of satisfaction for ourselves.

Those two themes began the process of thinking about the

homily for today. In the first reading we have a story of a call. It is one of the many examples of the call of God to the people. This time it takes place with a young man called Samuel. Samuel was like so many other individuals in Scripture. He was born of an elderly woman who was perceived to be barren.

Samuel was educated in the temple of Eli. Eli was his mentor and he was teaching Samuel all about life, the practical things as well as the religious things. Samuel kept hearing this call. He would get up and go to Eli's room, and Eli would say, "I didn't call you. Go back to bed."

It is a beautiful little tableau of the call each of us has. In the old days, before Vatican II, when we talked about vocations, we were talking about religious life or marriage. But since Vatican II, the instruction of the last 30 years has developed the concept of the call, the *vocare*, as it is in Latin. Today, the understanding is that we are all "called" people. We are all called in a vocational type of thing. We are all called to be part of the grand design of God.

So we read in the theology of today about the "priesthood of the laity," the "priesthood of the people." That's what we celebrate. I think in the years to come we are going to be celebrating this more and more. As has been said so many times before, the pendulum has been swinging from a clergy-centered church to the church of the people. I find it a very healthy swing of the pendulum.

It emphasizes that we are not passive recipients of all that the Church has to deal with, that we are called to be part of the great experience of God and Resurrection and Salvation and Peace. It all begins at baptism. Just as with our little Roxanne Wurth, who is being baptized today. Her parents have brought her to the community where the call will be issued to her to come forth, to develop, to become ultimately a conduit of God working in the world.

From the very ordinary experience of baptism, which we take for granted most of the time, and from the ordinary Sacrament of Confirmation, which we also take for granted, we become transformed into what Paul calls in the second reading the "temple of the Spirit." This carcass that is ours is nothing more than the covering that allows the Spirit to come into our world.

How else is God present to us in a direct way but through

each other, and through the Word of God and the Eucharist? Our existence takes on an entirely different message. And the message that I got on my candy wrapper points this out in such a simple, but beautiful way. *Notice the extraordinary in the ordinary.* Baptism changes us. It brings life to us.

It is unfortunate that so many times we don't recognize our body as a temple. Gosh, we abuse it, don't we? Last night, after I completed the 6 p.m. Liturgy, I thought about how good a pizza would taste. So I drove home in the snow. I parked my car. Then I called Clifton Pizza and was told I could come by in 35 minutes and pick it up. I was ready. I took my hat off but that was about all I did. I waited 35 minutes, got back in my car and picked up the pizza. I took it home. I put it before me. I got a diet coke and I started the celebration! This morning I rued the night and the pizza! But it was an ordinary thing, wasn't it? We do this to ourselves all the time. We don't always take good care of these bodies of ours. But the extraordinary thing about our bodies is the spirit. The spirit whereby we enter into relationship with each other.

The Gospel today is a very simple and yet detailed outline of the call. Picture, if you will, John and his two disciples standing there, watching people go by. John might have said, "See that guy over there. He is important. I think he is the one we have been looking for." The first element in being called is to have it pointed out to us, to be told that this is the person who will give us direction in life.

So the two men go over and they start following Him. He turns around and says, "Where are you going?" And they say, "Where are you staying?" They identify each other. They are now entering into the mystery of the call. Then the Master says, "Are you willing to go along?"

You and I don't know what is ahead of us, but we are willing to go along. By the way, I should have said this: that God has no respect for age, time, place, or mission when he makes the call. And it does not just happen once in our lifetime. It happens over and over again, that we are asked to find the extraordinary in the ordinary. And so they go. They enter into the mystery and they go along and they spend time with Him. They are enchanted by what they find. Eventually they leave and they walk off. Andrew looks for his brother,

Simon. "Come, Simon, come and meet Him. He is really something else!" They didn't know that he was God. They didn't know that he was Christ. Finally, He gets in the boat and comes over to Simon and says, "They call you Simon, but I am changing your name to Peter. Your name is Peter."

That is what happens to us when we open ourselves to the Spirit of God within us. We become the conduit for God and we are looked upon differently. We act differently. We are conscious of our own imperfections. But we allow ourselves to go forth and find the extraordinary in the ordinary. When we do this, then the concept of gift comes about. The gift—the opportunity that you and I have to give and to receive from other people. That's the gift that is spoken of in my candy wrapper: *The reward for a good deed is to have done it.*

Coming back on the plane from the retreat I sat down and was reading a book, *Sacred Silence.* It is about denial; denial in human beings, denial in society, denial in the Church, denial in our country and so on. And about how we choose denial in order not to look at the gifts and the opportunities that we have—the denial that blocks us from being conduits of God's grace.

There was an empty seat between me and the gentleman on the aisle. I looked at his book and it had pictures of boils on the cover. Eventually he looked over and said, "Where are you going?" I told him.

Then he said, "Are you enjoying that book?"

I said, "Yes, I am. It is a wonderful contemporary statement about the Church and its problems today. What are you reading?"

"Well, I am a physician and I give lectures on boils."

He was a pleasant gentleman from Canada. Our conversation went on, and I listened to him tell his story and explain his frustrations and ideas about where we are as church today, where we've been, and where we are going to go. It was an ordinary conversation. But it became extraordinary to me. So it was a gift.

I share these candy wrappers with you this morning as a basic thought for the vocations you and I have. We have been chosen by God to look for the extraordinary, and accept the opportunity to be conduits of God.

Expectations Versus Reality

Jeremiah 20:10-13
Romans 5:12-15
Matthew 10:26-33

Who can really live up to our own expectations? We have expectations about institutions, church and government. We have expectations for parents. Parents have them for children. Husbands have expectations for wives and vice versa. We really have expectations for everything that involves us. Yet, no one, no institution, no thing can really live up to our own expectations.

Many times we go through life frustrated because we say to ourselves, "If only I had so and so, or if only this or that would happen, then things would be better." But it's not going to happen. So there we are, frustrated. I don't think that is an uncommon experience.

For many of us, when we used to listen to the radio or watch television, we would find the ideal family settings. They were always the popular radio or television shows that told us about this father who was so dedicated to his children, and the wife who was so dedicated to her husband. And they all lived in the land of utopia. *Father Knows Best* was one of these shows. *My Three Sons* was another. *Ozzie and Harriet* was very popular at this time. Harriet would get up and say, "Good morning, dear. How are you?" He would reply, "Just fine, dear. How are you? Isn't it a lovely day? And here come the boys!"

Leave it to Beaver was another good one. *The Brady Bunch* was another ideal experience. Growing up with this type of mentality about how perfect life should be and then reflecting on our own human experience makes us realize that there is a vast chasm because our experience is so different from what is portrayed in these programs. You know, from the beginning of time, reality has never measured up to the ideal.

Take, for example, in our first reading, the story of Jeremiah. We refer to him as the Prophet. Yet Jeremiah was a lousy prophet. He didn't want to be a prophet. God *made* him a prophet. So what did Jeremiah do? He worried about what the public was going to say about him. The first half of the reading tells us that. He knew that they were murmuring against him. They were making fun of him. They weren't taking him seriously.

What Jeremiah really wanted was for the people to respond to him in an ideal way. He wanted to be accepted as the ideal prophet. He was miserable because that wasn't the way it was. He was miserable until he caught on to the fact that this was his own problem. And his problem was that he did not feel in control. He couldn't let the people be people. He couldn't see that his role was simply to preach, to teach. If they caught on, it was fine, and if they didn't catch on, it was fine also. But his role was simply that of being the prophet.

I hasten to say that all through the Old Testament, no one liked prophets, because prophets always spoke the truth. Who among us likes to hear the truth?

So here is Jeremiah. Finally, the Spirit of God came upon him and straightened him out. God said to him, "Jeremiah, you don't have to be the most popular prophet that ever walked the earth. Just do what I ask you to do, and everything else will fall into place." Once Jeremiah got that idea in his mind, he was all right. Then he understood. Then he went on and did what the Lord wanted him to do. He was relatively happy in doing it, I think.

In the second reading today, Paul is trying to explain something to us and it is in sort of garbled theological language. You have to read that passage several times in order to understand what is being said. I think Paul is saying that sin, as it is referred to in the Old Testament, is the total concept of selfishness. You know, we have to have things our way! It all started with the story of Adam. Adam and Eve had to have things their way. They couldn't allow God to play in their world.

Then, "in the fullness of time" as scripture says, Jesus came along with a different message. It was a message that was diametrically opposed to being selfish. It was a message of love. "Love your neighbor as yourself." "Forgive." "Don't carry around a burden of resentment for people who don't live up to your expectations." "Forgive, and live life." This is the message that Jesus brought to us. This message is just as real today as it was at the time of Christ when he was preaching.

Today we celebrate Father's Day. I've always had a hard time with Father's Day and Mother's Day. Not from the standpoint that I loved my mother and my father, and I certainly respected their sacrifices on my behalf. But the problem came when I went to get a card for either one of them. I don't know that Gibson and Hallmark have ever come up with an appropriate card. On second thought, I'm not sure they could ever sell any cards if they did come up with the appropriate card. Let me give you an example: I remember a card with a little old white-haired lady knitting and sitting in a rocking chair. She had a cat curled up on the floor near her chair. And there was a basket of yarn on the floor. The card had "Happy Mother's Day" on it. I realized I couldn't give that card to my mother. She is not white-haired, she doesn't knit and she hates cats! This is the card that I'm supposed to send to convey my love and respect? No!

So I wrote Mother a note. It was more honest. It wasn't manufactured in this plastic world that we live in, of *Leave it to Beaver*, or *Ozzie and Harriet*, or Mother's Day and Father's Day cards. I never found a card that was suitable for my father either. No card had a case of Falls City Beer on it! So I had to make up my own card for my father. It was a *real* card.

What do we celebrate today on Father's Day? I think what we really celebrate is the gift of life. I think that we have the opportunity, in a special way, to express gratitude to our father or our mother, who, in an expression of love, made it possible for us to come into existence. Regardless of what else they did for us in the course of time, the most valuable gift that they gave to us was the gift of life. If they lived up to our expectations, or if they didn't live up to our expectations, that's okay. The ball is in our court now. We, as the product of this experience, have the opportunity to continue the message that Jesus gave to his disciples: to share love, to accept forgiveness, and to give forgiveness.

The Gospel then tells us one thing. It tells us that we are not just simply accidents. That we were created in God's image and God's likeness. And God knows every one of us. You read about "the hair on your head" and "the sparrows falling from the tree." God knows us just as we are. When God sees us, he loves us. And my friends, that prompts us then to do the next right thing.

So my suggestion to you today as we celebrate Father's Day and meditate on the readings of the day, is to let go of the expectations that we place on each other. And *live* the message of Christ with each other. The message that is so human. The message is not calling for us to be perfect. But the message calls us to love and forgive and do the next right thing.

Highway to the Sky

Wisdom 3:1-9
Romans 5:5-11
Matthew 5:1-12

One of my favorite authors is Flannery O'Connor. She has a wonderful ability to sort of get in under the mask and the skin of the individual. She wrote a book in 1956, entitled *Everything That Rises Must Converge*. If you were to pick that book up, I would recommend that you read a short story called "Revelation." It is a perfect story for today, as we celebrate the Feasts of All Saints and All Souls.

It is a story about a woman named Ruby Turpin. Ruby, in her own estimation, is far beyond the ordinary woman. Because of her good disposition and manner of living she was well aware of others and their difficulties and plight in life. She would do anything for you, whether you were white or black, lunatic or freak. Also, Ruby considers herself the pillar of the community. She and her husband, Claude, are "home and land owners." Ruby thanks God everyday that her mother did not raise an idiot!

Ruby also has put most people she comes in contact with into one of many "categories". And she only associates with the right people. She doesn't cast judgment directly on anyone. But she certainly has her own very strong opinions about people.

Claude and Ruby support themselves with the proceeds from their hog farm. So one evening, Ruby goes out to feed the pigs. All of a sudden, just at sunset, she had a vision. (That is why the short story is called "Revelation.") There in the sky was a great purple streak, and then she could see a highway emerge and it seemed to be extending into the dusk. She raised her hands in a profound gesture and a visionary light settled in her eyes. And on this highway were herds of souls, rumbling toward heaven.

When she looked more intently, the people on the highway were people whom she knew. First there were the "white trash" as she called them, and they were followed by "black" people in white robes. They were singing and dancing as they moved along. And behind them were the "lunatics" and the "freaks," shouting and clapping. Then came the people whom she felt comfortable with, you know, people like herself and Claude. She leaned over to look closer at them. They marched behind the others with great dignity, and they alone were singing in the right key! However, these people had an expression of great surprise. They could see their own "virtue" sort of mingling with all the rest.

In a moment, the vision faded but she remained where she was, immobile. She eventually made her way up the darkening path to the house. In the woods around her there were the usual birds, but she didn't hear them. She only heard the voices of the souls climbing upward into the starry field and shouting hallelujah.

Now I share this story with you because on this feast I thought it would be good for us to stand beside Ruby Turpin and look at life as God perceives it. There are two things Ruby discovered. First of all, she was amazed at how universal God's world is. Second, she saw it as totally ecumenical. On the other side of the grave, there is no room for biases and prejudices that separate people from each other. There will be no distinction between black and white, rich and poor; there will be no one labeled freak or lunatic. There are no Democrats or Republicans. There are no straight bishops and gay bishops. There are no women priests and men priests. There is nothing that you and I hold on to that separates us from others. All will be one in the Great-God-Soul who calls us to life eternal.

God brings us into this world and then takes us through death into everlasting life. And there is really no place in God's world for bigotry, for prejudice, or the smallness that we may hold on to as we live out our lives.

Wouldn't it be wonderful if you and I could start this process of change, or purgatory, where we are purged from all the stuff that keeps us from being really loving people? Wouldn't it be different if we lived in a world where we had no regrets? That is the challenge of the story of Ruby Turpin, because sooner or later, everything that divides us will be purged, according to Flannery O'Connor.

There is something about celebrating the memorial of the deaths of loved ones, friends and acquaintances that is, in a way, frightening. Every once in a while there will surface in our own particular experience the thought that "if only I had done this or if only I had done that." We sometimes live with regret. Regret that we didn't have the opportunity to be with an individual when he died, or that we didn't tell her we loved her, or that we didn't tell him we were sorry. For some of us, we carry this regret for the rest of our lives, unless we do something about it.

I'm suggesting that there is a way we can do something about it. We begin by looking at ourselves and being able to eliminate some of the bias and the prejudice and the blame and the shame and all the rest that we ourselves carry around. We can do this with the help of others, like a spiritual director, for example. I have found in my own experience that it is possible.

About 10 years ago I was having a session with my spiritual director and there surfaced an issue I had with my father that I had not resolved before he died. And the spiritual director said, "Well, why don't you do something about that?" In retrospect it really wasn't a big issue at all, but that was what I was feeling at the time. So I said, "What should I do?" "What I would suggest is that you go to the cemetery and talk to your Dad in his grave."

Time passed and finally I decided I would go to Dad's grave. But I needed to do it in my own way with all the help I could get. At the time I was addicted to caramel ice cream, so I went to Graeter's Ice Cream and got a double dip cone and drove on over to Newburg Road. I went to the family grave and sat there and ate my ice cream. I looked at my father's name, my mother's name and my name. Then I started to think about this issue that I had come to discuss with Dad. All of a sudden, it was gone.

It was just gone! I found that I had nothing to say. And then my thoughts turned to prayer. And I started thanking my father for giving me life, for providing a good home, for loving my mother, for seeing me through college, graduate school, and the seminary. I thanked Dad for taking us on vacations and showing us other places in our country, and for many other things he did for me. It was strange. These gifts just sort of surfaced in large bold letters before my very eyes. My prayer had become a prayer of gratitude, thanking God for this man, who had given me all these things, and who walked with me and had given me counsel, who had corrected me and who stood by me. And my prayer ended as my ice cream cone ended. Ever since then, I have no doubt that my father walks with me, as well as other relatives who are gone. It makes me feel very blessed.

This process that you and I are in called life is oh-so-temporary and oh-so-short. When you and I die, the souls that are on that highway to the sky will change. One of those great souls will be united with another great soul, and eventually they will all be united to the Great God Soul for everlasting life.

And that is the meaning of the Mystical Body of Christ. It means that the Body of Christ is present in this community, as it was with those who came before us, and as it will be with those who come after us, in freedom, love and respect.